Hiram E. Butler

Exoteric Christianity

Darrell Jordan, MPS

H. E. Butler.

Hiram E. Butler portrait hand-drawn by Jessica Naomi

Hiram E. Butler Exoteric Christianity

Compiled with graphics and edits by Darrell Jordan, Copyright © First Edition 2023. All rights reserved.

No part of this book may be reproduced in whole or in part without the written permission from the publisher, nor stored in any retrieval system or transmitted by any means, electronic, mechanical, photocopying, recording, or other, without the written consent of the publisher.

For bulk purchases, please contact the publisher.

Enquiry@Athenaia.Co

Library of Congress Cataloging-in Publication Data

Names: Hiram E. Butler | Jordan, Darrell

Title: Hiram E. Butler Exoteric Christianity

Description: First U.S. edition. | Coeur D'Alene, Idaho: Athenaia [2023]

Identifiers: LCCN (pending) | ISBN 979-8-88556-047-4 (First Edition hardcover)

Subjects: OCC016000: BODY, MIND & SPIRIT / Occultism | HI036000: PHILOSOPHY / Hermeneutics | OCC014000: BODY, MIND & SPIRIT / New Thought

LCCN record available at https://lccn.loc.gov

On the internet: Parallel47North.com/collections/esoteric-books

Managing Editor: Darrell Jordan
Original Author and Essay: Hiram E. Butler
Executive Producer: Yuka Jordan
Book Cover Art and Illustrations: Jessica Naomi
Image Credits: Hiram E. Butler's personal collection
Printed and bound in the United States

Publisher: Athenaia, LLC
2370 N Merritt Crk Lp, Ste 1
Coeur D'Alene, ID 83814 , The United States

Hiram E. Butler

Exoteric Christianity

Darrell Jordan, MPS

CONTENT

INTRODUCTION	11
MAN AND HIS CAPABILITIES	13
Delivered to the Society of Esoteric Culture, Boston Mass. 1887	
THE POWER OF CREATIVE THOUGHT	24
Delivered before the Society for Esoteric Culture, of Boston 1887	
WHO SHOULD STUDY ESOTERIC SCIENCE	36
A Lecture delivered before the Society for Esoteric Culture 1887	
IN HIM WAS LIFE, AND THE LIFE WAS THE LIGHT OF MAN	46
THE MYSTERY OF SIN	58
Delivered before the Society for Esoteric Culture, of Boston	
GOD RULES	67
Delivered before the Society for Esoteric Culture, of Boston	
I KNOW I KNOW	78
Delivered before the Society Esoteric of Boston	
THE MIND OF WISDOM	88
Delivered before the Society of Esoteric of Boston	
UNITY OF DESIRE	97
THE DEVELOPMENT OF THE RACE	102
Delivered before the Society Esoteric of Boston	
IMMORTALITY; CAN IT BE OBTAINED WITHOUT DEATH	111
AN OPEN LETTER	
SUGGESTIONS OF THOUGHT FOR MUSINGS	113
SIGNS OF THE TIMES	117
FAITH IN GOD	122
THE COMING KINGDOM	129
AUTHOR AND MANAGING EDITOR	135
BOOKS BY THE AUTHOR	136
THE ARTIST AND ILLUSTRATOR	137

INTRODUCTION

Hiram E. Butler was born in Onieda County, New York on 29 Jul 1841. After a stint in the Army, he had migrated to Boston in 1885 for a short time wherein he gave lectures on a variety of metaphysical subjects to the Esoteric Society of Boston. Butler would not remain long in Boston and had moved to Applegate, California.

There, he founded the Esoteric Fraternity on a five-hundred-acre homestead, building an 18-room house for him and his fraternity members in 1887. They established a farm for self-sufficiency as well as a printing press.

Butler published several interesting books such as "The Seven Creative Principles" and his most recognized work, "Solar Biology" in which he simplified astrology by basing horoscopes on sun and moon signs.

We have compiled his speeches to the Esoteric Society of Boston as well as some papers he wrote on various topics, sprinkled throughout. We found his work quite interesting in an exoteric sense and believe it would be just as interesting to the general public.

Butler passed away on 3 Nov 1916 in Applegate at the age of 75.

Darrell Jordan, MPS - Managing Editor

12　Exoteric Christianity

MAN AND HIS CAPABILITIES
Delivered to the Society of Esoteric Culture, Boston Mass. 1887

The psalmist asked the question, "What is man?" The same question has been asked by the reasoning mind from the earliest historic times. In our own age, we, too, find ourselves asking this question. It is a question so deep and comprehensive that when we are perfectly able to answer it, we shall be able to answer the question. What is God? From its very nature, it must therefore be dear to your minds that, even were we to pursue this question throughout eternity, we could not reasonably expect to find its full solution.

The triangle, as symbolizing the trinity of being and as expressive of man's threefold nature, has been used from a very remote period. First, is symbolized the spirit, the father, or origin of being; second, the body or the nature formed by the spirit; third, the soul, that which is created by the action of the spirit on the body. Accordingly, the ancient pictures representing this idea contained the father, mother, and son, or Osiris, Isis, and the infant Horns.

Many of the ancients entertained the idea that matter, and God were equally eternal; that the former was just as much without a beginning as the latter; and that these two eternal principles were parallel to one another. They believed that man's existence was caused by the descent of the spirit into the flesh, into earthly conditions, and that by passing through different earth conditions he finally gained an experience which prepared the earth element to receive the astral fluid, and that out of this fluid a soul-life was ultimately formed. Hence the astral soul or body.

But I do not profess to belong to that class of individuals who believe in the eternity of matter. There is too much evidence that matter is transient; that it may be transmuted from one state into another, until, at length, there is evolved from the coarsest matter the finest spiritual essence.

The fact that there is not a particle of matter in existence that cannot be changed into gas, that cannot be so sublimated that it will cease to appear to the eye, is of itself evidence that it is of a gaseous nature, and that it was in the form of gas in the beginning. Of course, the finest senses are unable to trace it beyond that point. Yet it is entirely proper to assume, if such an element can be evolved from the gases, that there is a law that is capable of carrying on the work of transmutation still farther, and, in fact, to any extent.

But, however variable or susceptible to change matter may be, you should bear in mind that God is not so; that as he is spirit, he is unchangeable, is the same yesterday, today, and forever, and is the ultimate essence of all being.

But the fact that we find every particle of matter in a constant process of change is evidence that it is full of life. It makes no difference what form this or that portion of matter may be in, we always find it full of life. It is by virtue of this life that it is ever at work, changing its condition.

From this I conclude that, if God is spirit, he created everything out of himself, and therefore matter; and consequently, that all that emanates from that source is like himself. All is spirit, everything that is, is spirit. The coarsest matter is his spirit, but it is a specific condition of spirit.

All matter is not in the same condition. For example, we strike the solid iron. It is solid and dense, and as it possesses these qualities, we cannot pass our hand through it. In other words, it is matter to us. But suppose we take that iron and cause it to pass through various stages of transmutation until finally it reaches the form of gas (which can be done), we can then pass our hand through it without feeling or seeing anything. We take food into our body to nourish it. It is solid; it is material. That food is in the laboratory of the body, and is, as it were, in a fire, where it is passing through the several chemical transformations which eliminate therefrom that which is of use and which will strengthen and sustain the body; some of this food is thrown off, but the greater portion is retained. As the physical organism is in perpetual motion, and as not a single particle of it is ever at rest, simultaneous with every thought and movement there is an electric current going from the will, through the muscles, and brain, which current burns out some of its material, and thus finally transmutes it into thought-essence, and into the thought that is silent, or that is expressed. This thought is as dense to the thought realm as matter is to the sense-realm. For example, I have known parties to go into the thought-realm and become utterly unconscious of everything except thought. I have been told that while they were in such a condition; they met other persons, or the souls of others, who had once lived on the earth. In fact, they declared that those souls were material and as real as anyone in the body, and that the ground on which they stood was as solid as our earth is to us. In other words, the realm of thought was a matter to them. But if we were to try to take hold of one of those former residents of earth with our hands, it would pass through them; it would completely elude our grasp. They would seem to be nothing whatever to the hand. It is, however, none the less matter, for all that; but it is in a different condition from that which comes within the observation of the five senses.

In continuation of what I have said on the thought-realm I may say that it has been known from very remote historic times that the only thing that makes us conscious entities at all is the thoughts we have entertained, and which are springing up in the brain. But, as all thought is made up of experience, it follows that without experience there could be no thought whatever, as far as man himself is concerned. This consideration forces us to the further conclusion, that thought is caused by the operation of the same law or by the same transmuted potency of spirit that creates and controls the body. Thus, you will see that the back of everything and running through everything is spirit, and that the latter is the substantiality of all that is.

If this be so, then man in his interior consciousness is spirit. But where in the world today is there one individual who is really conscious of being spirit? Do you realize the significance of the term spirit? The consciousness of being spirit is equal to the consciousness of being God, and such a consciousness is infinite in its nature. It is what I might term an all-consciousness. It pervades all things, cognizes all things, and is everywhere. It annihilates space, destroys time, and causes the past and the future to become merely one eternal now.

In view of such a thought, we are compelled to say that there is not one who has come to a consciousness of spirit. It is true that we have all attained to various degrees of soul-consciousness. But you may ask, what is this soul-consciousness? It is the ability to take cognizance of thought like itself.

At the present time, we hear a good deal said about psychometry or the power of measuring soul, or that power by means of which one soul measures another. Now, I maintain that it is not proper to use the word psychometry in any such sense. The term that should be used to denote such a power or the action of such a power is psycognomy. It has reference to that refined, enlarged, mature, and exalted condition of soul which has been attained by passing through suffering and trial through the many phases of life, and especially by coming in contact with our fellow-men. Such a condition the ancient Magi and Oriental masters enjoyed, and the powers which they possessed, in consequence, are spoken of by theosophists as the ten senses. He who had the tenth sense was regarded as being in the God condition. Accordingly, there was in this sphere the sense of sight and the sense which beholds that which transcends the sight, and which spiritualists term clairvoyance, or clear-seeing; the sense of hearing, and that which hears sounds that transcend the natural ear, which spiritualists denominate clairaudience; the sense of feeling and that which senses objects that transcend feeling, which power spiritualists have improperly named psychometry, but which I designate by the word psycognomy. Again, there is the sense of taste, and that power which transcends the taste, and which has to do solely with the tasting of spiritual essences or qualities. We are also told that there is, in addition to the sense of smell, a sense which transcends everything of a material nature, and that has to do only with spiritual aroma, with sensing the pure and impure conditions of persons. These powers, they say, belong to the soul, and are even independent, to a great extent, of the senses of the physical body.

The nerves connected with the five senses respond to the physical vibrations of the atmosphere and the surrounding chemical conditions. These are the senses in which the whole animal world is living at the present day. The only difference there is between man and the rest of animate things is that his senses are finer, and of a higher quality than those of the beast. Of course, man has a soul, by means of which he is able to comprehend the nature of his environment, to invent instruments, and adapt means to ends in such a manner as to gain an advantage over his competitors in the struggle for existence. For all nature is in a state of warfare, — all living things being in combat one with another. During this struggle, which has been waged from the remotest epochs down to the present time, what is called the secondary brain was formed.

It is in this secondary brain that five of the ten senses reside. One of the remaining senses is in the middle or center of the brain. Two of the transcending senses are in the body, while two of the same kind of senses are in the brain. In the snake, the only thing that can be found to represent the brain, or nerve center, is a little gray matter which lies just the back of the head. Man was once in the same undeveloped state. But by unceasing effort and struggle, and working from as well and towards the center of his being, he has risen out of that low state of psychic existence into what he is today; has formed for himself a body that will serve him in action and respond to the demands of his will.

This process of development, of rising out of the lower into the higher conditions of life, of working outwards and upwards from the center of being, was undoubtedly the reason why the most ancient astronomy, as represented in the solar biology of the time of the sons of Jacob, began to construct the grand man with Libra, as if that was the first psychic formation.

But I would modify what I have just said. I have reasons for believing that the construction of that man commenced before the time of Jacob. It really began with Virgo, and sometime between August 22 and September 22, because at that time the calendar began with July 22.

This association of Virgo with the building of that grand man has reference to the element of pure nature; it relates to chemical qualities. It is preeminently the chemist. Consequently, one who is born under Virgo is the natural chemist. It represents that element which receives the food into the stomach for purposes of nutrition, and which eliminates whatever is necessary, and then carries on the important work of building the physical organism.

This was the kind of work which they did in the golden age. The people of that time learned through inspiration what was the divine law of being, — that such was the case one has only to examine the great pyramid of Cheops. Notwithstanding, the world has made so much progress in material things there is evidence in that pyramid that man in that remote and wonderful age understood the law of his being as he has not since.

It is clear, then, from what I have said thus far, that the spirit-essence resides in the function of life, in the reproductive or creative function. This fact undoubtedly suggested to the people of that age the propriety and reasonableness of commencing their year with the sign Libra, which represented that function. Here it was where first the divine spirit took up its abode in humanity. Here in the reproductive function, God first resided as the creator, the originator of man's being.

Now this function of the human organism and of the solar plexus impelled man irresistibly to strive to invent instruments by which he could supply the wants of his body. To this end he was provided with hands and a brain, with the reasoning faculty, which power relates to the five senses or to the things of this world. For this faculty has no reference to anything except method. It relates to the quality of life as a principle of action. In other words, it has to do with the quality of life-action. In either case, it is the same thing. For the quality of the life is the quality of the action, and vice versa. When the quality of life has attained a certain degree of refinement man is able to think like his author. In proportion as he is bound to the earth and to the things with which the physical senses have to do is he forced to act like the lower animals which are devoid of spirituality.

This brings us to the question of self-culture. That we may enter upon such a culture and move towards our ideal where shall we begin? We must begin to increase the quality of the life-essences. Whatever will improve that will bring us more into the interior, and thereby bring us into more intimate relations with ourselves as well as into a knowledge of what we really are. On this account, I have in my previous lectures emphasized the importance of controlling the reproductive principle, of conserving the life-essences, in order that they may be transmuted into the highest spiritual energy. I have striven to impress on your minds the necessity of such conservation, because it appeared to me that in that way only could man refine the essences of his nature, move forward in the direction of his destiny and towards a perfect oneness with his God.

While this thought relating to the essence of life is in my mind, let me say one word in regard to incarnation. My view of the matter is something like this: These physical bodies of ours received their life-essence from the parental germ, and after passing through a long series of incarnations, not as persons but as essences, they finally became able to create for themselves a soul that will be immortal, and which will be ever conscious of its own identity. You will observe that I say the soul will be immortal, and not that it already is in that condition. For, in order to reach this desirable end, the soul must be brought into existence by a refining process of body, which must continue until the senses are capable of taking cognizance of eternal realities. Out of this consciousness of eternal things will come forth a mature consciousness. In other words, there can be no such thing as an immortal soul, an entity that will ever continue to be the conscious ego, until man, by the process active in his own body, has refined the essences of his being, has enlarged and intensified his susceptibilities to such an extent as to be able to see and feel the infinite life, the eternal thought, the potencies of spirit, with as much clearness and certainty as he beholds physical things. The great trouble with us is that the powers of the soul are so dull and unrefined that the spirit is altogether too subtle for our perception or discernment. We move hither and thither in the world, and this divine essence passes through us as through a vapor, and we feel it not; have no consciousness whatever of its having touched us, or of its existence.

Now, there is a method by which we can be refined and made more capable; for the spirit of God is a consuming fire and burns on the altar of reproduction, and in this way this power may be so transmuted, its essence so directed into higher spheres of utility, and the quality of this life-power so improved, in consequence, as to supply us with the ability by which we can recognize divine realities and attain to a realization of God. This is the only way by which we can obtain immortality. We must begin with the very source of life itself.

We must change the direction and quality of the currents of our being. This was the idea which Jesus had in his mind when he said to Nicodemos, "Except ye be born again ye cannot see the Kingdom of God." Out of that declaration of Jesus sprang the idea of regeneration, or doctrine of the new birth.

Again, that germ of being which began our life was the highest essence that man could receive at that period. It was the perfect essence of paternal and maternal life. Of all things that are, it was the nearest to the spirit. It has undergone many changes. It has passed through first one transmutative period and then another until now it appears as fire. This fire it is that manipulates and controls the body, and is, in fact, the animating principle. Here is a principle, and nothing more. It begins to grow and expand, and in the course of time it attempts to perform experiments. The fires are active in their nature, but as yet, they have not experienced any such thing as development. The time for that has not yet arrived. Although the fires are active in germ, nature has so contrived as to make it impossible for them to come into being, or to manifest themselves, before a certain period.

As soon as that period is at hand, solar fluid enters and dominates our bodies. This same fluid is that which forms the intelligence of brute creation. This spark of life was drawn from life itself, from the earth; in a word, from the very substance of things. It is then taken by the seven creative principles, and used in accordance with the peculiar function of each. As I have already intimated, until a certain period, this spark exists merely in germ. It is in all of us at birth, but it cannot be observed.

The child comes into the world, acts out its childish nature, partakes of first one kind of food and then another, is nourished and grows. What do we mean when we speak thus? Simply this: the body extracts from the food that which it requires and causes it to pass through the different stages of transmutation, after which it ceases to be material, assuming as it does the quality of thought-potency. As this process continues, man begins to regenerate himself and, at length, stands forth in possession of all the powers and possibilities of manhood. Such a man is what he is through the transmutative process of the body and the generating of those elements which are indispensable to the support of the physical organism.

A certain philosopher has said that there is a power that comes from the astral fluid, and through the medium of the astral body which it created; and that this power sustains us and prevents anything from being lost.

Such a statement, however, can only be true in the sense that all sustenance comes through the operation of the seven creative principles, which principles are really active under each zodiacal sign.

But the truth, as far as man is concerned, is that nothing is retained beyond the period of use. This is the case with our thoughts, which are thrown off and never recalled. In a like manner, may we speak of our various experiences, which are forgotten. This is the law of soul-growth. Were it otherwise, the soul would be encumbered with a useless mass of material and would be unable to make any progress. In fact, we see the same law prevailing in the vegetable world. A seed is cast into the ground by the husbandman; it takes root and grows, and presently two small, delicate leaves make their appearance. Before long two more tiny leaves are discovered, shut up, as it were, between their elders, and peeping just above the parent stem. Very soon you see the first two leaves drop off. They have done their work, and must make room for the newcomers. In this way, that seed keeps on growing. Two little leaves are ever springing up from the center of the stem which it has developed, and ready to take the places of the old ones which have served their purpose and been cast to one side. In a similar manner, does man grow. He is dropping his surface life. This is the case with the one who grows rapidly. The same may be said of us so far as we make any progress at all. For the greater the celerity with which the soul throws off the old, the sooner does it enter into the new conditions, and the greater is the rapidity with which it grows towards the infinite. It is the aspiring soul that is forgetful. The live man is ever forgetting the past and reaching out into the future. Like the plant, he is growing continuously from the inner; is ever casting aside the old and the useless and developing the higher and finer part of his nature.

But, notwithstanding our experiences have been forgotten, they have not been lost; for our thoughts are as literally our children as those which may have been born to us in the flesh. They come through the same process and are material beings or essences. But, although our children are also material beings or essences, they may become immortal; they may attain to that soul growth by virtue of which one makes himself an undying entity, while the thought-children, devoid of physical body, must return to their original elements or be reincarnated in some form of life.

There is a vast amount of difference between a progressive soul and one that is bound up in the past or in the affairs of the world. There is a great difference between the power of the soul to hold to its own conscious being and the mere power to hold from disintegration. It is true that which is disintegrated is not lost; but it does not remain with the individual, but necessarily goes to the spheres where it belongs. It may have and has other uses elsewhere. Indeed, the astral fluid above us is filled with experiences, not only of men who once lived on this earth, but also of higher intelligences which have entered into nobler realms of soul-life. Such intelligences are like the tree that is ever rising into the heavens, ever reaching after the light, ever aspiring after and grasping the new. Such action may be said to be characteristic of one who has come to a consciousness of his own being; for this immortal element is made up of a tendency to reach ever after the infinite, and an exactly opposite tendency to let go one's hold on past experience. As soon as the soul ceases to manifest such tendencies disintegration and death necessarily follow.

Such a view it was which caused many of the philosophers of antiquity to liken man to a tree, the roots of which were in the heavens, while its branches were on the earth. Its growth was represented as beginning in the heavens and its blossoming as taking place on the earth. And is not the origin of the soul in the heavens, and will it not reach maturity and perfection through the material elements of earth? Does not the symbol suggest that which ought to be the tendency and ideal of the whole human family? I think so. What, then, is the course we should pursue? It is to allow nothing to prevent us from moving forward, but to keep our eyes steadily on our ideal of God, to the end that we may all become conscious parts of that tree which has its roots in the heavens and the branches of which, even though they may be widely apart at times, still form one tree, being united as they all are in the same trunk. It is the consciousness of a common origin and a common destiny which alone can bring men together.

This thought may be illustrated thus: I take six balls, which have been attached to a string, and then drop them on the floor in front of me. When I want those balls to come together, all that I have to do is raise the string and they conform immediately to my desire. One instrument draws and binds them together in common. So long as they are held by the string they are not easily thrown out of position or out of order. But suppose I should take six balls unconnected with any string, and I should drop them on the floor, though I might succeed in bringing them together, yet the least jostling would throw them apart.

So is it with men. They are flying off in a tangent, hither and thither, unless held together by the string of some grand and common idea. Hence, I regard that soul as greatest, which keeps its attention fixed on its highest idea of God; which keeps its aspirations after God constantly alive and fresh. Such a soul will know no limit to its growth; it will rise higher and higher continually; will be ever throwing off the old and unfolding the new, and ever gaining deeper and higher and more comprehensive ideas.

In proportion as we enter this higher life of the soul, we discover the fact that we are only a part of this spirit essence which appears to be subject to matter, but which in reality makes the latter, through the principle of transmutation, the instrument by which it accomplishes the loftiest purposes imaginable. In fact, the higher we rise in the realm of spirit, the more conscious do we become, and the more able are we to enter into the mind of the infinite. Having entered into such a state, we lose sight of our narrow and contracted material individuality, and arrive at that consciousness, which is the consciousness of God, the consciousness of all things at the same time. Thus, you see, although one's individuality may be lost in the infinite whole, his consciousness is not lost, as he has a consciousness of all conditions, of all being, of all thought, and of all spirit.

THE POWER OF CREATIVE THOUGHT
Delivered before the Society for Esoteric Culture, of Boston 1887

This afternoon I will take the second chapter of Genesis, 4th and 5th verses, as the basis of my discourse, wherein we find the second description of the order of creative energy. The words Day and Night have a broader significance than the revolutions of the earth upon its axis every twenty-four hours, and in the Hebrew, properly rendered, would imply "periods," not days, as we understand them. In this chapter, you will observe there is a repetition of the account, with slight modifications. In the 5th verse we have these words concerning what the Lord God created: "And every plant of the field before it was in the earth and every herb of the field before it grew, for the Lord God had not caused it to rain upon the earth, and there was not a man to till the ground." You notice in this text the declaration is made that the Lord God created the plant, the herb of the field before it grew in the ground. Our friends in the church, as well as ourselves, — for we in the past were not an exception, — though we may not have been intimately associated with the church, having been thinking independently for years, we may, therefore, have grown so as to think a little more in harmony with the laws of nature than in our early lives; but at one time we thought that the Lord God was a great man, who, judging him after ourselves, had gone to work as we would have done, and made the plants out of some element, or had made elements from nothing, and thus formed the plant preparatory to setting it out in the ground, or caused it to be placed in the ground to grow there. You see, of course, this is the logical conclusion, judging the Infinite Mind by the processes and methods of our own daily avocations in life, and the habit of our daily thought; that when we have attained a deeper and more comprehensive idea of God, had obtained a knowledge of him like that which was possessed by the Cabalists or prophets of antiquity, by the and there of the Bible, who clearly taught throughout the entire book that God was everywhere present, — not beyond the limits of "time and space," as some have chosen to sing, more than here in oar immediate presence.

Moses, in order that he might put up a barrier against the children of

Israel making to themselves the image of a man to represent their idea of God, and limiting his nature, principles, and methods to that image of a man, by inspiration gave them this commandment: "Thou shalt not make unto thee any graven image or likeness of anything that is in heaven above or in the earth beneath or anything that is in the waters under the earth. Thou shalt not bow down thyself to them nor serve them." The habit of the past has been to make images of God like to ourselves, and we have thus interpreted that passage where it says, "And the Lord God created man in his own image; in the image of God created he them," etc.

We have laid hold of this statement with great pleasure, because it enabled us to form an image of God and place it before our mind's eye, that we might have the image of a man to bow down before. Great efforts have been made by philosophers to do away with image work, and to present to the human intelligence an idea of God as a spirit that pervades every particle of space, and that is as much in this room as in any other place in the universe, being that all-pervasive essence of life, from which, and out of which, all things came. I know this is a difficult thought for the ordinary mind to grasp, but any person who chooses, for a time, to live the life that is necessary, — that is, isolate himself from the business world, going away into the solitudes of nature to muse upon God, the Creator of all things; allowing the interior and psychometric faculty, if you please, to go from vegetation, from animation in its varied forms, to the contemplation of God, — will find after a time that he will obtain a consciousness and power, a perception and sight that will enable him to realize clearly and distinctly this subtle essence of life, even as he does the objective things of this physical world.

When such a consciousness is obtained, we will have quite a different realization of the idea of God. We will then perceive, as we move along through life, even as I move across this platform, that the divine essence of being from which I derive all my consciousness, all the attributes of my nature, all that I am and have, and all that there is in the world, is in this very element through which, as we would ordinarily say, I move backwards and forwards. But the consciousness obtains in this case that we do not move through this element any more than this element of life moves through us; and the only impingement or consciousness of this divine essence of being that we have, is that degree of spiritual essence or entity that we have obtained through the process of regeneration.

To whatever extent we have matured spiritually, to that extent we sense the touch of the divine essence of being, and are thereby conscious of the realities of the existence of God, the spirit and soul of the universe. Before obtaining this consciousness, — which no one can do save by set rules, and methods through which life may be developed, spirit consciousness matured, interior consciousness refined, concentrated, and ultimated into a consciousness of God, — no man can intelligently and effectively pray to God.

Therefore, Christ taught by two distinct methods. One was the esoteric line of instruction which he gave to his disciples apart from the multitude, and the other was the line of exoteric teaching that he gave to the public. He, however, imparted much of the esoteric teaching in parables, that the common people could not understand. He said to his disciples, "To you it is given to know the mysteries of the Kingdom of Heaven and unto them it is not given."

Why? Because they were not willing or ready to receive and practice them. It was for this reason, and not from any idea of caste or exclusion. But to them that were ready to receive and practice the esoteric doctrines Christ gave those teachings, and with the teachings he gave the endowment of the powers that he himself possessed, and with which, after his time, they were enabled to heal the sick, raise the dead, cast out devils, and do the works that he himself did in life; but the multitude who were not capable of receiving the esoteric teaching could not do these works. The same is true of the teaching of pure Christianity. It must continue to have, as it certainly always has had from its earliest period, two lines: one to the general public, and one to the chosen few. Chosen by whom? Not by another. The chosen few are those who adopt a course of life that makes such teaching practical.

I wish to present a few Noughts in connection with what I have myself experienced regarding the laws that relate the soul of man to the soul of the universe, that we have heretofore called God. We are told by the teachers of antiquity that God is unchangeable, the same yesterday, today, and forever. If this be true, then no prayer, no anxious restless desire on the part of mortals, can cause him to deviate from the set rules and course of his own divine will. Yet all the wise men of ancient as well as of modern times have taught us the great necessity of prayer, remembering not only its usefulness, but the necessity of praying in the words of the Nazarene, "Our Father who art in heaven. Hallowed be thy name, thy Kingdom come, thy will be done in earth as it is in heaven."

"Pray" always, "without ceasing." Now this may seem vague, impossible. But what is prayer? Prayer is the sincere desire of the heart. What is meant by the heart? We have heard these words a great many times; but what do they mean? Who can answer that question? We find physiologically, through the new method of delineating character that we have recently published, that the heart is the source of love, zeal, and emotion; of the essences of the spontaneous higher and purer nature that brings forth the earnest desires that we meet in our daily lives. Then prayer is that interior anxious desire that springs forth, by natural volition, from a realization of a need that must be supplied. There is no other way or method; only by reaching out toward our highest ideal of God, and gathering from that source the object or essence of our desire, or the power to obtain the thing desired. What takes place at such times? It does not change the Infinite. No; but if your eyes were opened, and you could stand at a distance and see what was taking place when a truly anxious prayerful soul was reaching out in earnest desire for certain results, you would be astonished at what transpired in that person's surroundings. They would appear like a great ocean of infinite life, and as he thus stood in this ocean of God-essence, the thought-forming power of his brain reaching out, you would see forming in that ether above him the thing he was desiring. Perchance it might be that a mother was thus praying for a wayward son. If that mother were in the true soul of devotion, you would see a luminous form being shaped in the divine ether. Ton would also see emanating from that mother's innermost and highest essence of being a luminous element, a life-essence going out from her to the object that was forming, and clothing that object with her own life, endowing it with all the functions of the child of her prayerful desire, thus making it in thought an embodiment of a God-inspired ideal. She has formed this image and clothed it with her own love-life; for I presume there are few of you here but know that when the heart is opened and your love goes out with an overflowing feeling for any person or object, that there is actually an essence of your own life that goes out from you to the person of your thought, and that beloved one will feel the warming influence of the life-essence which is flowing from that devout soul.

Thus every emotion, every feeling, that emanates from man or woman partakes of their life-essence, goes out into this ocean of life, lays it under contribution, forms it into images of their deep desire, which are clothed from their life-substance, and endowed with the potency of their wills, as illustrated in the case of the mother to which your attention has been called, who, by her own magnetic life and will, created, as it were, an angel form to pervade and strengthen the soul of her son, wherever he might be; and whatever intensity there might be in that devout mother's breast would find expression and act upon that wayward child according to the intensity of her desire.

In every case in life, wherever true soul-prayer is offered its powers obtain in the invisible world. So likewise with the very thoughts that pass through the human mind. It is well known that every thought we have partakes of the essence of our being; that in connection with all thought there is an electrical current which goes from the organ of will into the brain or into the body, and wherever that electric spark comes some part of the body is burned out, transmuted into a subtle element of energy or of thought that goes out as a part of our being, having been formed by the imaging power of oar brain; for you know that we cannot realize a thought unless that thought has taken form. An unformed thought is not intelligible; not a thought can exist without form. Now, by this thought-forming process of our lives, we are peopling this solar fluid, this solar ether, that we are passing through, or which is passing through us, as we move along in life; we are peopling it with thought-formations from our own lives.

We are told that God created the world and all that is in it by the word of his power. These words were thought-forms, and this thought-forming process precedes the physical form; and when these thoughts have taken form, they go where the will directs them, let it be where it will. For instance, we have known or heard our fathers and mothers tell strange stories about haunted places and houses, where the image of someone that had lived and departed this life could be seen, where some person had lived and grown, as it were, into the place; his whole thought had been made up of those surroundings, the will had bound him to that house or place, and he could not or would not go from it, even when he had departed this life. Let a person that is sensitive go there, and he will see that shadowy form apparently occupied in the same vocation, and clothed the same, as it was in life. If, perchance, there was any peculiarity in the dress, it would appear. Whatever there was in life, thus it would still be seen; because this shadow-form is made up of the thought-forms of the person while alive, who was bound in that place, as the will had not allowed it to go beyond that sphere. So, our thoughts are controlled by our wills as to what they are, where they go, and what they do.

Every plant has in it first a thought formation. The thought that forms the plant gathers to itself chemical essences from the air and earth, and builds for itself a body whose essence, when elaborated by growth and concentrated in the seed, is again an epitome of the thought that first formed the plant; so that not only did the Lord God create by forming thought-essences in the beginning of the plants, the beasts, and the birds, but of man himself. And what was the thought-formation of God concerning man? Read the 26th verse of the 1st chapter of Genesis, and we have the expression of the thought that was in the mind of God, that took form, that began creation, and that is now working in all spirit, in all matter in this divine realm of the Universe, and that finds expression in the united forces and thought-creating powers of the moving body of the solar system; for the movement of the sun in its orbit and of the planets around it are producing thought-forms in the earth. And God said, "Let us make man in our image, and let them" — that is, the dual man that He created — "have dominion over all the earth." — be master. When the Nazarene came, he was master; he demonstrated this to the world, and said to the world, "If you do not believe me, believe the works that I do;" for the works demonstrated that he was here as the representative — as the man that was to be in the image and likeness of God.

In the solar ether, we have the essences of all things that appear in the physical world. All that ever will be on this side of life is first formed in the ether "above." Our minds are wholly dependent for their existence on this ether, which is their native element, just as much as the fish is dependent for its life on the water in which it moves. Could we be taken out of this fountain of divine essence? We would die as quickly as the fish dies when taken out of its natural element. Now, here is a great subject, and how can I best treat it for your comprehension? When I look out upon the stars above, I see the homes of a grand people; for the planets of our system are actually creating thought-forms of gigantic character, as recognized by the ancients, whose interior consciousness was opened enough to see and comprehend these aggregate thought-formations of moving worlds and systems. Nations of the earth are swayed like great seas hither and thither as by a mighty wind from the solar world. We look out into the world today and we find men and women starting out in some peculiar custom, and we call it a fashion. Some little simple thing is invented, and they all take it up; they follow it; some peculiar line of thought at certain times sweeps over the land like a tidal wave. There is just as much a tidal wave of human thought as there are tidal waves of cold, of heat, and of waters of the ocean. These tidal waves are caused by certain conditions of the planetary world.

Now, man is the expression of a thought, and that thought is the expression of the Infinite Soul. Life on this earth is subject to the influences and changes of this solar and boundless essence. Is there anything that we can do that we may become masters, and not servants? Is it possible for man to have dominion over the very elements and essences on which he is dependent for an existence? Yes, it is. But how, when we are as dependent as any creatures can be upon this divine breath, as we may call it, this divine ocean of life from which all the thoughts we think are gathered? Through that fountain, we are caused to think along certain lines by virtue of the aggregate conditions of the thought-forms of the heavens, and by them we are controlled; we are but little atoms, as it were, floating in the great ocean of life. To take control of that ocean in which we are, that seems like an impossibility when we look at it casually. Yet this is our privilege, when we can come to an understanding of those seven creative principles that find expression in our life, and use the power that we possess to create and control thought. Power is the likeness and image of God; God created worlds by the thought-process, by taking of this life-essence, concentrating it, forming it, sending it out by the will, to be and do according to the will of the thinker. Every time you form a thought, you gather the life essence of the body into the brain, form it in the brain, and send it out by the will to be what you have willed that it should be. This was the process of creation. Here is the likeness that you and I bear to the Creator, — the ability to create thought-forms and send them to do our wills. By this creative process that you, and I, and every living thing possesses, we take hold, through our physical bodies, of the material essence of the world; through our intelligence, of the solar essence or fluidic ether; and through our spirit-nature, we take hold of the spirit-essence, or infinitude. By the proper uniting of all these in the trinity of being we may create in our own individual selves any condition that we please, so that these bodies, this mind, and spirit animating them, can control, change, and concentrate power and become as gods individualized, by partaking of this God-principle.

We can project, with this spiritual ether, an organism into being and nature like to that of which we are the expression; we partake, concentrate, inspire, fill ourselves with it, bind it within the elements of our own magnetic spheres, confine it, subject it to our wills, and cause it to obey as we send it out into the ether to do our bidding, so that when we have regenerated ourselves by the presence of this God principle, and have got control of the thought and generic process of our bodies, we will have control of the spiritual essence of our natures. We can then create out of the spirit-essence of God whatever forms we please, clothe them with our own life, as we do our children. It is a more sublimated life in this case; yet in this manner we become creators, and create thought-forms, and they are our children as literally and materially as the child that is generated of the flesh.

Thus, we see that the processes of the mind are generative and creative processes, and that all things have their beginning in thought-formation. How do I know this? By giving me the date of the birth of your child I will tell you just the mental conditions that were guiding your minds as parents prior to conception, and from that I can tell you all about the thought that is incarnate, and will express itself under certain conditions in the mind of your child all through life. As a trinity of spirit, soul, and body have united as gods, and have concentrated a spark of spirit essence, you have clothed that spark with thought, which is the soul; that thought in its proper position has gathered to itself and formed a material body, and thus come forth into life as your earthly child.

Now, when we look deeper, when we understand these interior and more potent laws of mind, we merely change the process thus: In place of creating physical, material children we conserve the potencies, transmute them to essences of thought, gather the divine essence of spirit, form and clothe it with our life-essence, make of it a spirit entity, and endow it with our will. What is our will? Our will is the God-will that we have inherited from Infinitude. Without the consent of that will, we cannot move a muscle, no matter how small. It is will-power that moves every muscle. It is an absolute monarch, and you cannot do the slightest thing without its consent. You derived that will from the great fountain of thought that wills to act out its own nature. You say I can do whatever I will to do. But what can you get the will to do? Now, the will is an absolute monarch. That will is the ultimate of all that you are. It is a part of the infinite, and absolutely your master. But by virtue of unfoldment and regeneration any man or woman can elevate the will and be master of these things that now rule us, that we are now subject to, such as the vicissitudes of life, and can inspire from the higher and yet higher will until they reach the great center or cause of all their environments and by it control them. You cannot will to do this unless by virtue of a quality that you have obtained by growth. Therefore, it is safe to say, whoever has the will to be a master, can be. But who is willing? Are you? If you have the will that creates an active desire within, go to work. You can accomplish it. But if you have not the will and have no active desire, no amount of talking on my part would cause you to do it; because there is that absolute monarch, ruling every thought, every desire, every feeling, every emotion, and that absolute monarch is the Infinite Soul of the Universe, and that spark of will-power possessed by each is a part of that infinite Spirit by whose creative processes the earth and everything in it was formed and projected into being. Fish exist and swim in the sea by virtue of their nature and qualities. Birds fly in the air by virtue of their kind and quality. Man plods and labors upon the earth by virtue of his; and the same will is monarch of all. This, then, being so, what is the use of teaching? It is this: you can grow and unfold the divine will that is controlling the work of creation, and has bound you in this world of bodily habit, which habits may be controlled or changed by one that is able to gather of the thought of the Infinite Mind and increase the will. He can turn their course by applying the law, and obtain more power, thus causing or increasing an active desire to lead a more perfect life, which desire or prayer leads to the end in view.

I am, at this moment, creating thought-forms made of this divine essence, clothing them with my life, sending them out to you by the effort of my will. They, being made of immortal essence, are themselves immortal; and though you may repel them, they will live on and on in the ages until they will find somewhere a soul that is reciprocal with them, and will receive them, and they will become an active, life-giving principle in him.

Creative will is productive of thought-forms like onto angels that have not yet become men. They descend down through man, to the animal creation, and from that to the vegetable creation. There they have expression in plant life, so that we are placed upon the apex of a pyramid, as it were, standing for the Hebrew letter Yod which represents the right hand of divine power, the active principle or will, — by virtue of the law that all life aspires to that above itself, the highest order of creation reaching out and up to the Infinite Mind. The next lower order of creation reaches out towards them and so all creation, from water and vegetation and all animal life, from the lowest states to the highest order of humanity, is reaching out in aspiration to that above it, until we come to the highest order, which is aspiring and reaching to the very God. Thus, the ascending current is flowing from the lowest order of creation up through all higher into the world of spirit; and from that creative world, the divine essences descend by virtue of man's desires, which call them down, ensphere and incarnate them when they flow out to others below, and so on down, until they reach the very lowest forms of life. And thus, we see the current moving from center to circumference; and this is the pattern of the planet Earth.

In the temple at Jerusalem there were represented four cherubs standing in its innermost center, spreading forth their wings to either wall, symbolizing the overshadowing of the earth. Then between them was the Shekinah, or presence of God, whence the priests received words of instruction to guide the people.

Thus, the Shekinah stood at the very apex of life, on the topmost point of the globe, even within the veil, and thus symbolized the throne of life and power toward which all created things, even down to the lowest forms, were aspiring. We are now standing just without this veil, ready to enter. We are on the topmost round of physical life, having within us the divine and quickened will, having it in our power to reach out and gather the very essence and substance of God's life, calling it down and giving it embodiment and expression, thence handing it down to others, and they in turn to those below than, until it reaches the lowest stratifications of existence. Thus, when we take hold of the forces of our being and have dominion over the body in all its functions and powers, we shall stand where the Nazarene stood when he said, "I will take of the things of the Father and show them unto you;" and thus may we all become instruments of service for the elevation of mankind.

The following question was submitted and answered at the close of the lecture:

Q. I would like to inquire whether you deem it absolutely necessary for a person to withdraw from the ordinary pursuits of the world in order to secure the cultured life that you have mentioned?

A. I do not deem it necessary that any person should permanently withdraw from the world in order to obtain that change I have referred to; but I do maintain and know that it is impossible for a man engaged in a business pursuit, where the mind is constantly occupied in his business, to obtain it without a period of rest. But one that wishes to possess these attainments can do so through taking control of his body, by a constant effort in that direction, and by keeping the mind centered on the ultimate object toward which he is aspiring. He may then grow rapidly, and soon discover that he has a separate interior consciousness that is capable of an entirely distinct line of thought and activity upon the subject toward which he is laboring; and thus, whilst man is engaged in the things of the world, he may have his inner consciousness engaged in the things that appertain to the unfoldment of spirit consciousness. But whilst he is continuously engaged in the external reasoning and business life, though that interior desire is ever kept active, he cannot come into the consciousness of the higher intellect, and see and perceive from a true scientific standpoint until he has, perhaps, his summer's rest, when he, instead of going to some place of amusement, goes out into Nature's quiet. There, alone with his God, he will be surprised, if he has kept his interior desire active, to see how much he has gained; and thus, he is encouraged, and goes back to his work, conscious of what he has obtained, and ready to go on growing from within; for we must grow as the flowers grow — from within.

WHO SHOULD STUDY ESOTERIC SCIENCE
A Lecture delivered before the Society for Esoteric Culture 1887

We have, in all the history of the world, had enthusiasts on the varied subjects of thought that interested the people of their time. Today, the subject of esoteric culture in its varied phases and under the various names, is in almost every one's mouth — words both for and against. No doubt we have many who are enthusiastic by virtue of the realization that they have of the importance of this interior subject of self-culture.

I often think of the words of the wise man Solomon; after he had investigated the whole realm of scientific and esoteric knowledge, he declared that he believed there was nothing better under the sun than that a man should be satisfied with the works of his own hands, for that is his portion. This I have often realized in my own experience. It is not a pleasant theme to pursue, in many respects, from the fact that, as we dive into the cause-world, through the development of the soul-power, which alone can reach out into that realm, we become conscious of the conditions of this world being hard to bear. We become dissatisfied with our surroundings; the conditions that otherwise would be those of pleasure and happiness, become conditions of dissatisfaction and displeasure. Therefore, there should be a careful discrimination made today, as much as there was in antiquity, and I suppose there is discrimination being made by the masters of the Orient, not to force upon any one thought that led out of the realm of this world's existence into another, unless there is some end to be attained.

But some of our friends may ask: "Is it not wise that all should develop the highest and best powers of their natures?" Certainly, it is wise that each should do so; but all have not grown to a condition where they will pursue this study far enough to be of use, thus doing themselves and the cause more harm than good. If we induce a person who has not reasoned above the plane of the ordinary society life, to look into this science, by holding out to him the beauties, the ideal pleasures that lie beyond, it only appeals to the material nature, and perhaps we might as well say the animal inclination that controls the world very largely to seek after pleasure in new and varied forms, which pleasure they seek to find through the senses. Thus, if we lead persons merely through the senses in pursuit of esoteric culture, we lead them into the realms of knowledge which become to them instrumentalities of evil, for they have not pursued it far enough to see why it fails to bring the beauty, or pleasure that they expected Therefore, we should be careful and present these thoughts only to those who are dissatisfied already with their present conditions in life. These words are found in one of the prophets, who warns us: "I charge you by the roes and by the hinds of the field that ye stir not up, nor awaken my beloved till he please." Of course, this language is figurative, and those represented as "his beloved" were those who are ready to reach out toward that divine source. Again, the "beloved" of God is the interior spiritual nature in man, and that we should not stir up nor awaken it until he please, is the thought.

Every creature will act out its own nature. Every man's and every woman's will is the quintessence of all that they are. That is to say, our will is the highest faculty of our natures; is the absolute monarch and dominator of all that we are. Now that will, through the reasoning faculties, may be changed hither and thither, but such changes are not good unless there is, already active enough in the mind of the person, a dissatisfaction with the present conditions of life, and a reaching out towards something higher. When we find such dissatisfaction in the minds of persons, we can very readily discover what cause is producing it; and then such persons as have unfolded in their interior life sufficient to be able to take proper cognizance, or to have a proper understanding of this interior, or spiritual principles, readily lay hold upon them and desire the knowledge.

Doubtless, the Masonic order was once the storehouse of spiritual knowledge; and I am informed that even to-day no man must be asked to join that society by one of its members. Such is also true of esoteric teaching. No man or woman should be asked to investigate this teaching until they have manifested in themselves the inclination to reach out after something beyond the ordinary sphere of life; and whenever they come to that point in their experience that they begin to desire that knowledge, because of their spiritual unfoldment and the conditions of the working world, relations become dissatisfactory and repellent to them, and there begins to grow a controlling aspiration toward the spiritual world. In such minds, then, the pursuit of esoteric thought will be advantageous, because it will be instrumental in producing happiness and satisfaction in their lives, whilst of course it may react on the lower plane of life and create greater dissatisfaction there; but yet when predominance has already obtained in the mind to create an active dissatisfaction, then they should have, and there always is, provision made that they may have this higher knowledge.

I presume there has never been a time when there was so much dissatisfaction as exists today, and I presume that seven-eighths of the people that are thus uneasy and dissatisfied with their present conditions and surroundings, are entirely unconscious of the real underlying cause of their dissatisfaction. But we see, as this wave — for it is like a tidal wave of spiritual and soul aspiration towards these higher truths — sweeps over the land, it affects all life. It is in the life-essences of the ether; and as man inspires from that divine life-essence according to his quality, this dissatisfaction is produced upon different persons according to their degree of spiritual unfoldment.

In my first lecture to this society, I made an effort to present my idea of God, and have frequently recurred to it because I deem it a very important thought, as it is that which underlies and overarches every other thought that the human mind is capable of taking cognizance of. On that occasion, I called attention to the fact that all we recognize as space is filled more densely than the densest matter with that very essence of life which, for the lack of a better name, a more comprehensive word, we call God. This life essence that pervades the universe is as varied in its qualities, in its nature, as anything that we have any cognizance of in the physical world. In order that a person may have the true unfoldment and soul growth, it is absolutely necessary that he should contemplate, meditate in quiet musings, upon the idea of God, that infinite, ever present and all-pervading life-essence. As we muse upon this subject, our own inner consciousness will be prepared to become the receptacle of that essence. But not unless we first rid ourselves of a certain repellent polarity that has been established in the human ego by virtue of the predominance of the law of self-preservation. This law has entered into every department of our being more thorough than we have any idea of. There is in every man's nature a weakness which subjects him to the psychological influences of his fellows so that every man and every woman is under a constant struggle to maintain their own selfhood, to carry out their own designs and to be themselves and not be lost in the great whole. This struggle that is going on in the external world is also going on in the mental realm, so that it is difficult for all persons that are thinking new and advanced thoughts to maintain their own definite conclusions without being interfered with, led off in this or that direction, by the thoughts and conclusions of others. This is brought out in the minds of the people by the idiosyncrasies and eccentricities of their natures. In our mother church where there is a united body, where they have agreed to concentrate upon certain thoughts that are accepted as foundation principles, which they have no idea of going beyond, they live each in the other's magnetic aura, and thus form a common magnetic body so that they do not struggle much and are safer and more at rest than any other people in the land. They can really enjoy life better than other people, simply because there is nothing to struggle for, save in their ordinary avocations. Whereas, if a man or woman starts out alone, to think for themselves, they find it as they would if they stepped out of a protected house into the prairie where the storm could sweep against them without anything to break its power. In such cases, if persons have any idiosyncrasies, they always come to the front; therefore, among the advanced thinkers of to-day we find the word "Crank," quite freely employed. Well, there are many of them, all one-sided, because, owing to the tendency to extremes, their arguments embrace the radical extreme of all subjects. Now the radical extreme of any truth is just as much in error as any other position that a man or woman can occupy. For instance, if I were arguing with you about some great truth. You would present your side of the subject, perchance one extreme, and I would be standing in the mean between the two. As soon as I began to argue with you, I would be forced by virtue of the power of words to go to the other extreme and bring thoughts from there to counterbalance yours that were brought from your extreme. Thus, before I was aware of it, I would be thrown into the extreme opposite, and so argue more radically than I believed. Thus, arguments become instrumentalities of evil to those who are striving for the truth. None can realize to what extent this is true until he has experienced in that direction and watched carefully his mental conditions prior to the argument and after the debate is over, because then he will see what change has taken place in his own mind. Although one may have arguments sufficiently strong to completely silence his antagonist, that very fact serves to intensify and lead him into more radical views than are consistent or true. Therefore, in everything that pertains to the struggle, to the combat man with man, thought with thought, there is an inevitable tendency toward extremes.

The wise Brahmin said, "I came not to teach men that which they do not know, but to teach them those things which they do know." This is the wisdom of a teacher of the esoteric science. Every man or woman that has come in any degree, into the consciousness of the Soul Universal, reaches out for a higher order or plane of life. But the life principle that I began to speak of a few moments ago, is only obtainable when all these barriers, thrown up by the peculiarities and idiosyncrasies of one's nature, are broken down by the only way that has ever existed or will exist to free ourselves from them, namely, by a Covenant with God. We have heard old people, when we were children, talking about witches selling themselves to the devil. I know I used to hear old people talking about these things when I was a boy. There is truth in this thought. A person has to virtually sell himself, soul, body and spirit, to whatever sphere of life he desires to become eminent in. While a man or woman stand in their own ego, and through their own will-power manifest their selfhood, they will find that they are in a constant struggle, a struggle that it is impossible for any man or any woman that ever lived or will live, probably, to maintain themselves in, and remain consistent with their own highest reason. Such struggles put up barriers against the unfoldment of the divine life that would otherwise flow in and take possession of them.

When a man or woman has meditated upon Life, has seen the great truth that it has mind, consciousness, all that has been attributed to God, and that our ideas of a personal Deity are absolutely true, that there is an independent thinking, conscious intelligence that takes cognizance of, and reciprocates with every sympathy, every motion, and with all human intelligence as well as with life everywhere; therefore, when man enters into a covenant with that divine intelligence, he at once rests in that covenant. He says, "I desire more now than all else in the world to be an instrument under the controlling power of that divine Mind." This Mind will be according to your own highest thought, let it be what it may, for every man makes to himself a God, whose nature and character are according to his own highest quality, by virtue of which he will when he lives up to his ideal, inspire constantly from that just a little above himself. And when he has entered into the covenant and seek like resting in it, he sells himself and belongs to God, and then will come the consciousness that divine Being does take control of his life. It will lead him, will instruct him, illuminate his intelligence and he has only to perform the duties that are laid before him day by day.

In that attitude, we are polarized, all our barriers are virtually taken down and we, through that confident faith in that infinite source, have around us a protection that others do not possess. There is an illustration of this before the people of Boston as before no other people in the land. The ideal of Christian Science, Mental Healing, etc., is wholly based upon that as the foundation idea. Now when we have entered into that covenant with the infinite soul and rest in the confidence of that covenant, we shall be guided and led in the way of truth, and shall realize that it becomes a truth to us.

I have often heard the quotation, "As a man thinketh, so is he." That is true. Whatever a man thinks, that he is, providing he believes it with all his heart, for whatever we believe without a doubt, we are. Now this belief that has no doubt in it may lead us to wonderful extremes. We have no idea and cannot have until we investigate the world of mind, to what extent that may lead us. I have seen persons, under the influence of another, psychologized so that he would say it was snowing and was very cold, when in fact it was very warm in the room, but while he believed it, it was true to him. Now if we can believe in this higher ideal of human intelligence, rest in it, confide in it, it becomes the essence of our natures, controls, guides and governs our lives, and we become it to the extent that we believe and rest in it without a doubt.

In my early experience, there was always active in me a desire to know more of the cause world. As a child when I went to school I had no interest in books, and, in place of going to school, I often played truant, went to the woods, wandered by the creeks, and spent my time in the fields. I delighted in the study of nature, in all its forms, and especially in insect and animal life. I grew up without education; yet, my delight was constantly to know the laws of nature, to know the producing cause in everything. After I had arrived at about the age of thirty, my mind was then called out of the old channels of the Church, and I first saw that the Bible prophecies were not all yet fulfilled. I began to study, and, with that simple childlike desire active in me, ever desired knowledge for its use. For some reason, from the time that I was a little boy with my mother, I remember well often saying to her, "I believe that I have a special work to do in the world." Now, whatever truth there may have been in that, this much it has done for me. It has kept my highest desire to that one object that I might be prepared with knowledge, with understanding of the laws of nature and the laws that govern human life, and the causes of the evils and sufferings that exist in humanity, the ways and methods by which each human mind could rise out of those conditions of suffering and evil, and attain the condition of happiness, health, and higher life.

As I went on studying and thinking, my attention one day was called to the words of Jesus, where he says: "Unless ye eat my flesh and drink my blood, ye have no life in you." I had always had an ideal in the Church of what that meant; but it came over me forcibly that morning, there was still a meaning there I did not know. I desired earnestly to get to know that meaning. That afternoon I was sitting in a little hall, in a meeting carried on after the Quaker plan; and while sitting in silence, suddenly I was conscious of their coming into the very center of my being a new life that permeated all my veins. It seemed to me as if an electrical fire went to the ends of my fingers, and every part of my whole body was filled with a new life. I was led to say, with the greatest emphasis, — "I have immortality; this body can never die." As I look over the pages of the Bible — for I always loved them, and do yet — I find these words (Ezekiel xvi. 6): "When I passed by thee and saw thee polluted in thine own blood, I said unto thee, in thy blood live; yea, I said unto thee, In thy blood live." I realized that a thought, formed from the Soul of the universe, out of the very essence, of Divine Life, had been sent into the center of my being, and from that time to this I have been enabled to reach out and gather of the knowledge that belongs to that cause world. Now there is a great body of people throughout this land that have had similar experiences to this, whenever their need and use was made manifest.

From that time forward, whenever I could isolate myself from surroundings, and sit quietly looking out in musings upon God, I have been conscious, more conscious of that divine life than I am of this world and all that we call material. This experience is not mine alone. Many others have become conscious of this divine life acting upon them. These persons are scattered over our land; we associate with them daily. In 1878 I had then begun living for some time the life of a recluse, waiting until I could see a door opening before me to go out in search of the people that had received this interior life, — that had awakened to the consciousness of the infinite soul. But no way opened before me. All seemed dark. One evening I felt oppressed, sad, and discouraged, and, from the depth of my soul, said, — "O my God, where are the people that we are looking for?" Suddenly, everything changed around me. I seemed to be somewhere overlooking the world. I saw the natural sunlight shining upon the people. They were all busy with their own affairs of life; but here and there was a dark place, where this natural sunlight did not appear to penetrate; and I was impressed to peer into these dark places, and, as I did so, I saw, first vaguely, the outlines of persons; and, as I looked more intently, I saw other persons, though right in the midst of the people, running hither and thither in the natural world, yet they were in darkness and obscurity, relatively, as to the affairs of the outer world; and the spirit said to me: "These are the people." These are the people who, though they are in the world, are not of the world; though they do their duties, walk like those around them, yet they are not of the world. To these people comes this new light. To these alone, not to those that are satisfied with the affairs of this world.

The ultimate to which we are calling your attention, towards which we are laboring, is to bring about a new world where the people will be prepared to live under the controlling influences of the Infinite Mind, having conquered selfishness, hate and passion. When these are conquered every cause of inharmony and combat man with man, every struggle in life, will have been destroyed. This ultimate will be a person of whom we may say, in order to bring it to the comprehension of the ordinary mind, that they will be as it were "psychologized" by the Infinite Mind. That is, their whole thought, their whole desire, and all that they are or hope to be, will be so linked to the Will of the universe that their wills and the Will of God will be absolutely one.

Now, to whom could we go to find any hope of such a condition? To none but those who have awakened to the consciousness of this divine life in themselves. Now this consciousness has come, as I said, in varied forms to each one different, but one general tendency obtains always, namely, these persons have with them the Spirit of Truth. This, as Jesus said, "will lead them into all truth." Error they are ever ready to repel. Truth they are ever open to. They perceive and know it when they hear it.

We have no need of fear about listening to this, that or the other, about going and investigating this phenomenon or that. We can go where we will, can see all things, can know all there is to know; and as we go around about the world, we can see everything, be ever ready, like the discriminative magnet, to gather the very essence that we need and repel all else. Therefore, we have no cause to be anxious. If we allow anxiety to enter our minds, that anxiety brings evil results, and breaks down the protective barriers. There is no motor power in the Universe but the Infinite Will. The storms that sweep the heavens are controlled by that Will, as is my hand as I move it to and fro. All worlds, centers, and systems, are held without a wavering or deviation, by the irresistible power of that Infinite Will, and when our will is one with that of the Infinite, then all power in heaven and earth is within us, and we can say with the Nazarene, "All power is delivered into my hands in Heaven and Earth."

Questions.

The following questions were asked and answered at the close of the lecture:

Q. Is there any power in the spirit to ward off what is called death?

A. Certainly. This is a subject that has been agitating the minds of a large body of people for many years. I refer particularly to those people known as Adventists, who have many names and many different branches. Among them, the idea has been prominent that there was a time coming when they, as to their bodies, would no more see death. Now, my position in regard to that is the same as it is in regard to every thought that obtains credence in the minds of the people. There is a truth in it. We read in the Bible that Elijah was taken up to heaven in a chariot of fire. Josephus tells us that Moses was taken away in the same manner. The apostles tell us that Jesus, after his crucifixion, was raised from the dead. Now, I believe that those people who receive the spirit have in them immortal life. I do not say all of them have it in sufficient degree to overcome the death of the body; but many of them will come into the order of the heavens where they will be free from the struggles of the astral world, where they can live in harmony with this divine essence that they possess; and to these persons, no such thing as dissolution of the body by death will come. But some will say, will they always remain so? No; but life is fire; God is a consuming fire. As these people live more in harmony with God, their bodies will constantly get more and more under the control of the spirit. They will go on refining the body until it is so spiritualized that they can stay on earth if they will, or they can dissolve the body and go to the other planets if they desire, or ascend into the heavens; so that which we call death will be overcome in such persons.

Q. Can a person in this life have an idea of previous existence?

A. I have met numerous persons who claimed a remembrance of prior existence, being able to state where and when they lived, who they were, etc. I can say for myself that I have, in a few instances, been as conscious of having lived before as I am of living now, therefore, I have great reason to give credit to those who claim a memory of prior existence.

IN HIM WAS LIFE, AND THE LIFE WAS THE LIGHT OF MAN

The subject announced for this afternoon is one of greater interest to the world than all other subjects. In the first chapter of John's gospel, we have these words: "In him was life, and the life was the light of man." The peculiar characteristics of John's teachings, and the history that we have, are such that they have led all the philosophers of modern times to unite in saying that John, the beloved disciple, was a great mystic, and many have allied him to the cabalistic school of philosophers. Let this be as it may, one thing is certain, that the subject of "Life" has been the corner-stone of all religious beliefs and teachings. One of the leading principles in the Buddhistic doctrines is, "All life is precious." We have all of us recognized that all life emanated from the one great central source. That central source has been brought before the different nations under different names, every name expressing the idea of the nation that worshipped before that unknown principle—Life. In the further teachings of John in his gospel, we find "God is Love," love being the phenomenon of our life on the feminine side.

Of all the teachers in the New Testament, no one has so fully as he chosen the theme of Love; that seemed to be the center round which all his thought gathered. We recognize in the studies of Life and its phenomena that Love is the leading characteristic, the main feature or leading phenomenon of Life. It is that principle that preserves, that sustains, that cares for and nourishes all its objects. Life is the primate and the gatherer of the material essences and elements that form bodies, of whatever nature or kind. The kind of Life, and the quality of that Life, always determines the kind of material and quality of the material that is gathered to form for itself a body, to be allied to the uses of this physical world.

John's declaration, referring to Jesus of Nazareth, "In Him was Life, and the Life was the light of man," only voiced the central thought in our Bible from Genesis down to Revelation. We begin our biblical history with the account of the first man and the first woman capable of receiving this higher Life, — not the first in the world, for immediately on tracing this history we find that the first offspring of that man and woman went out from them and married and raised children from other peoples, and soon after we find a denunciation made in that history against those children of Adam, who were called the "Sons of God" that married the "daughters of men."

There seems to have arisen at that time the ideal of a higher and purer order of Life than was in the world before. It is a law in Nature that nothing can act or think above its nature. Persons cannot attract or inspire thoughts that are not in harmony with the highest principles of their organism. There is not a principle in the world that has not had its expression in some living form. Everything that lives gathers to itself the elements from the sunlight, from the atmosphere, and from the earth, according to its need for the occasion, let it be what it will. So, in the progress of unfoldment of human life, as fast as men unfolded in their experiences to a point where there was something in them that reached out and produced a desire for a condition above that which they at the time possessed, the desire in itself was the first principle that led to revelation. For aspiration, which reaches out, gathers in the desired thought, which then acts upon the life forces, and the life forces react upon the brain, then the imagining power of the brain puts it in its form, and thus, from being taken cognizance of by the perceptions, it becomes a revelation to the intellect.

We find that Life has been ensphered by men in direct accordance with planetary conditions, and that the positions of the several planets have always expressed the nature and stage of unfoldment of the inhabitants upon our earth. Therefore, in the history of the past in every cycle there has come to the world some representative of how thought and light, being a revelation of new and grander religious views than those of preceding ages; yet some cycles have apparently been of a descending nature. We have but little of the real history of Adam, neither is it necessary that we should have more; but there is a history of him as a man in direct communication with the Spirit of God; and we find that he began to impress his life and experience upon the world, and through his posterity, his nature was multiplied. The history in Genesis bears evidence of residence from the Divine Nature. We observe him in the light and communion of the heavenly kingdom, but polarized in the senses, bent on experiment and personal experience, which culminates in the deluge or Noachian Cycle, which was the counterpart or complement of the

Adamic Cycle. There is a threefold law that controls the evolution of the faculties of the mind and the cycles of race unfoldment. The first and second are counterparts, or express the law of duality. The third is an interregnum, or transition. The three together constitute a grand unit or cycle. The fourth begins a new cycle, and has for its base the three preceding. The mathematical plan of the human brain is that of an ellipse (an elongated circle), with two focal points or centers, one for the back brain, the other for the intellectual hemisphere. The same law governs the evolution of historic cycles. The accompanying diagram represents the cycles from Adam to the present time:

No. 1 represents the ellipse of Adam; No. 2 expresses that of Noah, and is the complement of the previous; No. 3 is the Abramic or Mosaic, and is an interregnum or transition to a new grand cycle, which culminated in the Christian dispensation, which is represented by No. 4. This ellipse was completed about the year 1881. We are now in the commencement of the fifth or Messianic ellipse, which is the complement or fruit of the previous; and, as the fourth marked a departure on the ascending scale, its duality brings light, peace, order, and spiritual triumph, which will be manifest with the expansion and ultimation of the present or fifth ellipse.

The law of the faculties of the brain, their evolution, magnetic current, and relation to the cycles of human unfoldment, cannot well be dwelt on here, but will be set forth at a subsequent time.

Thus, we find the first historic period commenced with Adam and spread out through his descendants until the first ellipse was completed, which was simply the elaboration of the thought and polarity that was active in his mind. We know, and have proof beyond question, and I believe it is largely accepted, that children are always the incarnation of the active thought of the parents' minds prior to conception. So true is this in our experience in delineating character that, knowing the dates of birth of a family of children, we can tell the parents what general mental conditions controlled them during those periods; so that if the parents remained in one general routine of life, it will be manifest in the marked similarity between all the children, whilst if the life is one of diversity, the children will have diverse characters.

The leading characteristic or the leading thought of the people is the thought that grows and expands. Most of the revelations that were made to Adam in Eden were simply an inspiration of the thoughts of God, the Creator. Having developed up to the point where man was able to inspire and take cognizance of the thoughts of the Creator, he lived to a certain degree in harmony with them, and enjoyed the benefits of the law of the Infinite; and though he fell, his posterity ever kept before them the active idea of what they might have been.

Thus, that thought, which was the seed planted in their nature, became the active principle in them, creating its kind in their posterity, and it was ever before them as the ultimate towards which they aspired. But always in the history of the world, as nations and peoples increase in number their interests become multifarious, and through their struggles, combats, anxieties, and worriment's their minds are diverted from the central thought and life-giving principle on which they first started, and through which they first obtained their prestige above other people. Yet that condition obtained, and the few continued to reach out for and incorporate this principle of divine revelation or spiritual knowledge, which was repelled and thrown off by the others. As Jesus said, "To him that hath shall be given and he shall have more abundant; but from him that hath not shall be taken even that which he hath." And thus, the seed was kept alive, and it began to focalize again towards the center, the same as it had spread out in the circumference, thus giving us the first ellipse of the world's history.

At the end of this ellipse, we come to the time of Noah, and see the desolation and destruction which came upon those who had departed from the light. The symbolical figure of this period is that of a great flood. Then followed the ellipse of Abraham and Moses, — a transition period, when the world was being prepared for new and greater light, which ultimated itself in the Christian dispensation, thus commencing the first ellipse of a new triune cycle.

At the time of Christ's advent, he found the world in a state lower, darker, than it had been before or has been since. The priests were thoroughly selfish, had left the law of God, had ignored revelation, were seeking only their own selfish ends. In the midst of that total darkness, there was no man with spiritual unfoldment; as the Prophet said, "When I spoke, there was no man to say. Here am I."

At this point, we have the manifestation of John the Baptist. Perhaps it needs a little explanation here. In the beginning, everything originated in thought; that thought was the Life primate and the Life ultimate as the actor, but it was the Life primate in spirit form, the Life ultimate as the physical form. Therefore, when we speak of Life, we speak of thought in its active agency, in organic form. Now at this period, John came under the law, or as a concentration of all that had been generated of the true principles of divine thought wrought out in man's nature during the former ellipse. Next came Jesus the Nazarite. (See Numbers, Chap. VI.) And, mark you, this Christ could not begin his mission until he came to John and was baptized; and when he was baptized, then we read that the "Holy Ghost, or the spirit in the form of a dove, rested upon him and abode with him." From that time, John said, "I must decrease, but he must increase." Because that true divine thought that had been generated in the world, and whose vocal center he had become, was transferred from him (John), as a representative and end of the old cycle, to Jesus, the representative and beginning of the new. Thus, he became the Adam, as Paul said, of the Christian dispensation.

There are many people today who question if such a person as Jesus ever lived. We may, on some future occasion, take up a line of thought in which we shall prove, beyond question, that whether such a historic personage as Jesus, the Nazarene, lived or not, one thing is certain, — there was someone who did live, and embody in his own person the principles that we have held out to us today as the expression of the Christ. Otherwise, they could not exist, for mankind cannot have a thought that never had form and expression. Remember that, for it is worth your while to think about it.

Now, at that point in time, there was the end of an age; the conditions existing in the astral world that made it possible, yes, made it necessary, by the law of systems, that there should come into the world a representative of a new and grander thought than had preceded it. The wise men, the astronomers and astrologers of the East, saw this in the stars, and went and bowed before that new representative of the era that was to come. Today, we find that the Christian religion has been branching out in every direction.

It is spreading out grander and greater than any religion before it, extending its branches in every direction until the world is now nearly filled with the idea of Christianity. But what is that idea? It is as yet only the vague and uncertain realization of that life that was, so to speak, planted in humanity at that time. But in Jesus it had full expression, and was the true light come into the world. Now, what is light? If you had no eyes to see, you would have no idea of light, no idea of form, save what you would realize through the other senses. If you should come into this hall when it was totally dark, you would not know whether any one was in the room or not, at least so far as the sight of the eyes was concerned. Open the windows and the light would stream in and reveal the faces of the persons present. This is the effect of light; it enables us to see and know.

Now in him was life, and true life is light as well, for the kind of life determines its form of manifestation. Therefore, he said: "Believe me, and if you do not believe me, believe the works that I do, for they are they that testify of me." Again, he said: "The words I speak unto you are Spirit and are Life." Thus, his teachings showed us the way to obtain the power and dominion, that his works demonstrated could be ours by following his example; for life, light, or truth are something real, and consequently we are told that if we know the truth, "it will make us free."

I have been many times surprised, and again was this morning, as I listened to one of the eminent ministers of our city, while he referred to truth as if it were some abstract object that was away off somewhere beyond the bounds of time or space. Truth is the fact of the things that are; that is all; in contradistinction to the things that we may imagine. If I say to you, there is no person in this hall, that is false. If I say there are persons here, that is truth. There are two principles in truth, the facts of things that are and that which recognize them, i.e., the spirit. The physical sense is often deceived; but "that which transcends the physical sense is the spiritual, which is never deceived." Jesus had developed that sense which always knows and discriminates between fact and mere seeming. "In him was Life, and the Life was the light of the world." To get light is to come to the knowledge of the laws, principles, and methods of the world in their workings, and the relation we bear to them, so that we, as intellectual and willing powers incarnate, made by the processes and powers that we have active within ourselves, having come to the understanding of these laws, will lay hold upon them, appropriate, and cause them to serve us, in place of our serving them. For the true light is that which pertains to the knowledge of facts and causes.

What do scientists know of causes? There are men that will point the telescope to the planets and to the stars, and tell us how many miles they are from us, their orbit, etc.; men, also, that will take a plant, and tell us all its chemical properties; but, after all that has been done, what do they know about cause?

In the spring of the year the trees put forth their leaves, the grass comes forth, and all nature springs into life. By what law? None of the natural philosophers can answer. In them is life, and that life has power to gather to itself the elements of nature and form for itself a body; that it may gather through that body the essences from the sun-ray, the atmosphere, and the earth, and materialize them to form and bring it forth for the use of the work of creation in nature. Here is life, but life is not yet light, but dependent on light for existence. That life is only a material phenomenon. The life that we are laboring to obtain is that life that enables man through aspiration to reach out into the realms of thought, beyond the common uses of the physical body and its necessities of food and clothing, and gather those thoughts that will illuminate the mind, will give it power to control the forces of nature that now control us, that we may no longer be subject to the law of sin and death. The Bible thought from beginning to end is that man should be "saved." The saving from the law of sin and death is done by virtue of knowledge and practice of the truth. That truth, then, relates to the laws of life and its relations to nature and to matter in all its forms and phases. The Nazarene came as an expression of that, and so was Light embodied. The diseased of every character, those possessed of demons, and the insane, were cured by his word. Again, by his word the winds and the waves of the sea were calmed, and a fish caused to bring the tribute-money.

Here, indeed, was a new Adam, a true man, causing the winds and waves to obey him, and even the fish of the sea to pay tribute. The wild and unchained forces of nature had found a lord and master in whom there was a life and light that gave knowledge and power over nature and man. The same thing, to an extent, has been claimed by all the mystics. We read that Elijah called fire from the heavens; that he commanded the clouds not to rain upon the earth, and they obeyed; and again, he commanded the clouds to rain, and the rain came and watered the soil. The same thing is accredited to the Hindoo masters today. There has not been a time in the history of the world, with the exception of a few dark periods, when there were not representative characters who possessed a measure of such power.

When Jesus came into the world, he found it in a most benighted state, and restored the departed spiritual light and power. The apostles for a time had this power to heal the sick, to raise the dead, and do the wonders that he did by virtue of having "learned of him;" but as they went on, they began to neglect these principles, and seek control. We will illustrate the idea as a ball, upon the apex of which the highest order of mind exists; as we go out from this, branching out in all directions are the lines of life in their evolutionary process. In the outermost lines, we have merely the animal use, whose material essences are subservient to those of the higher order in the innermost; so that at this point, and by the action of these higher minds reaching out and inspiring from the divine, they bring down this higher thought, clothe it with their own magnetic life, and it goes on and on down the line, until it gets where it finds no expression save in negation. The Christian church of that day received the divine thought of the Master in its purity. Each branch has had some sacred truth that it has nourished and cherished. Some have claimed that this divine life that was in Jesus and made him the Christ, pertained by inheritance, and was transmitted from the father and mother to their children, and therefore there was a right of inheritance to the church. This was true, for they had the true principle of life active in their intelligence at that time. But they have gathered round that truth a multiplicity of errors that made that truth suitable to their conditions. Just as the farmer plants the seed in the ground, which germinates and grows from the decomposing and corrupt matter with which it is surrounded, just so these divine principles were planted by the Nazarene in the nature of earth's children, which was his material church, covered by all the errors and filth of their animal natures; yet these germs have grown. Now, in the churches, we find that multitudes of people are talking about the love of Christ; but just picture in your own mind the Nazarene, that man of sorrows, one acquainted with grief; that meek, humble personage, that was not admitted only as he went in by a dominant will into the temple where the people worshipped; that despised man who gathered around him fishermen for his disciples, — imagine that man to-day coming here and going into one of our fashionable churches. How many there would say, "Hail, Master." How many there would not say, "Here is a tramp; let us put him out, we do not want him here;" and especially if he attempted to teach those divine laws of magic. If he were to come to them and teach them those higher and grander truths to bring them back to the true principles, how long would they tolerate him? Not very long, I fear.

There are people in the world that have these divine truths in their hearts and in their lives, and can develop up to this life that was in the Nazarene. The life that is to be the light of the world is the life that we want to see gathered together; and we want to see men unite their thoughts and their efforts, and get an understanding of its laws, and their relation to the planet earth, to all the planets of the system, and to the creative forces that are acting upon our lives. And, as we come to understand these, the next important step is for them to get control of their bodies, so that they may stand out in that mystic name, — that name that was hidden by the priests in the time of Jesus, and put into the ark where no man could see it; and the priests themselves had a saying, that anyone who pronounced that name in its proper letters his name should be taken out of the Book of Life. Why? Because that was the key-note in the Book of Life, namely, that name given in mystic language, Yahweh.

Some years ago I was in Springfield, and there met a Jew, a very learned man, who said, "There is one thing I do not understand. In my own language we have always been taught to call this word יהוה , answering to YHWH, Adonai and Elohim; but it does not spell that." There are few Jews to-day that do understand it, because they have been taught by their priests not to pronounce it, because its meaning expressed more than they wished to assert; to express that name is to say, "I WILL BE WHAT I WILL TO BE."

For a man to express that name, and mean what he says, is to "take the name of God;" and to step out and say to the laws of Generation, "Though I have been subject to you all this time, by you I came into existence, by you I am, now I know you, now I am your master; therefore, you shall no longer drag me down, destroy my humanity, for 'I WILL BE WHAT I WILL TO BE.'"

Who dares to take that position? Who dares to step out into this rushing tide of waters of generative life, that is rushing down toward the great ocean of forgetfulness, — step out in the midst of that rushing cataract, and say, "I will go no farther; I will no longer be driven down into the great ocean of nonentity, but I will be the master of these forces"!

In thus doing, we come into the control of the forces of dominion. Now, if there is any one object for which Jesus came into the world, it was to teach men that in them was this divine power, this divine right, like that One Moses said "the Lord thy God would raise up," that should go before his people as their leader; as the One referred to that had "the name of God in him," that could stand in the power of that name and say, "I will be what I will to be." That divine right is also ours.

John writes, "In the beginning God said, Let as make man in our image and like us, and let them have dominion over the fish of the sea, the fowls of the air, and over all the earth." We are now under the dominion of those laws and forces that are and have been carrying us down from generation to generation, from father to son, and from mother to daughter. Death has been in the world, and we have been subject to it. But I know this is a large subject. Death is in the world to-day; but will it always be? I think not. Jesus says, "If you follow my teachings, do as I bid you; you shall not die." The Jews at that time did not believe it any more than people do on this day. But it is just as true in the natural sense as it is in any other, and I state here, by the right of Divine Sonship, by virtue of that power that exists in you and me, and by the light that is in you, in connection with the knowledge now accessible, of the law and forces that act upon and control your own physical bodies and mental conditions, — that by ruling them you may produce in yourselves that perfection of Life, that no matter what comes, though this body might be crushed into atoms instantly, there would not be one instant of unconsciousness. You can, without difficulty, get to that point by standing out in your humanity and saying, "I will be what I will to be."

It is for this that we are talking to the people, and have organized here that you may learn and understand those methods, and apply them, to enable you with others to stand in your right as the sons of God and be what I will TO BE.

The following questions were asked, and answered at the close of the lecture: —

Q. I would like to inquire if you think there is power enough in every individual to be what he wills to be?

A. There is not power enough in the individual in the ordinary sphere of life; but, if he knows how to get the power, that power is in his reach so that he can be whatever he wills to be. That power is attainable. Those of you who have read our first lecture on the idea of God know that we are among those that see God everywhere; that in my hand there is enough of God, the Infinite, to create a world, even within the limits of my fingers, give it time enough; and when we have taken of the substance of the world and by the processes that operate in our own bodies transmute and etherealize the essences until they have become a vessel to gather and hold the divine essence that passes through us now as though we were but a shadow, then we will begin to have that dominion and power that will not only rule this body, but the forces of nature, so that you can by those processes be whatever you will to be.

Q. Do circumstances alter or change the effect?

A. We can, if we will, have dominion over circumstances. But here is just the point. If you have the will, — there is where it all hinges. To have the will to apply the law, to proceed in the methods and accomplish the results, to have enough of that divine principle and to lay hold on it and let go everything else, and pursue that one thing until it is accomplished. The man or woman who has enough of that tenacious holding quality in him or her can accomplish it.

Q. Are we not like the fruit tree, requiring a certain condition for the growth of the spirit and divine life in us to have those attributes, and divine light to perceive and use them, in order to be what we will to be?

A. Yes, but there are a few scattered over the world who have developed up to that state.

Q. Does it require a certain fulness of time?

A. We are just what we are, and have had just what time we have had, and those among us who have come to that point where we see these things see that the power is in our hands.

Q. Is not the requisite a perfect trust in God?

A. It is a perfect confidence arising from knowledge. I think I should rather call it faith, from the definition of faith by Paul, who said, "Faith is the substance of things hoped for and the evidence of things not seen." By a properly cultured life, we obtain certain evidences, and from results which follow, we derive unbounded confidence from within, which is faith; so, then, if we proceed further, certain other results will be accomplished, which are further evidences; thus, faith will grow and strengthen with every attainment. Now, we may, by the proper appliance of the laws that we have been teaching here from time to time, get the substance that will give us the faith that will enable us to lay hold upon that unbounded will, and incorporate within ourselves the power of that name, "I will be what I will to be."

Q. Have we got to obtain this substance, or is it already within our reach?

A. The powers are already within us to reach that substance, by application of the energies that we have. The only thing is this: We have now certain faculties; they are limited by virtue of the limitations of our knowledge; in beginning, with what knowledge we have to study these laws, we must begin at the very beginning, as the child begins with his A B C's.

THE MYSTERY OF SIN
Delivered before the Society for Esoteric Culture, of Boston

The mystery of sin? Yes; for it has been a mystery since the time man began to think reasonably and logically upon the idea that all things emanated from one common source, that source being one of all goodness, wisdom and power, and yet that we should find in our world this principle that we call "sin." How can we reconcile to our minds the mystery of its existence? We look out upon a world of disorder, of sorrow, of misery, of intrigue, of injustice, of falsity, of crime, all apparently emanating, at least permitted by, an infinite mind.

We have been told from the beginning that sin was the transgression of the law. What law? God's law; because there is no other. It is well to discriminate in our own minds between the statutes of men and the laws of God for, if God is the Creator of all things, of all forces, of all principles, then all true law, of whatever nature or character, can but be the emanation of that divine mind. When we take a view of the world of creative energy, and form in all its variety, we think we see therein inharmony, chaos, and disorder. We see it thus because we judge of all things from our own personal consciousness, and from that point of view we condemn all things as evil, — as sin, — that are not in harmony with our own ideas and desires. Were we capable of rising to the sublime heights of the mind which rules the universe, which projected it into being, set all things m order and place, and had in its original thought use for everything that lived, we would then see and understand the great mystery Paul referred to when he said that "All things work together for good to them that are called of God, according to his purpose." From that expression we see readily that if all things work together for good to those who are living up to the infinite purpose of the Creator, then all things become good, and evil vanishes away and ceases to exist.

Good and evil are necessarily relative. We say, from our standpoint, each and such a thing is good. Why? Simply because it serves the uses that we wish to be served. We say that such-and-such things are evil because they oppose us in the accomplishment of our aims in life. Therefore, the terms adversary and adversity become virtually synonyms; also the words, evil and devil, become synonymous and both of these belong to the same family. Anything, whatever, that is in harmony with our purposes is considered good. Let us illustrate. We see a man become very angry with his neighbor. He forms a purpose in his own mind to injure him and he matures a plan by which to accomplish it. You, being a just man, and wishing to save the neighbor from the injury which is planned against him, step forward and endeavor to thwart the carrying out of the evil design. You at once become to that man an adversary, and your efforts to thwart him seem to him evil and a sin against a law of right which he has set up in our own mind, and, in turn, your ideal of right, being superior to his, his efforts are of evil import to you.

Thus, the combination of circumstances, we may say, forms two evils, each adverse to the other; for both are evil, allowing each individual to speak from his own standpoint. If evil were absolute, it would dethrone the Deity. There is such a thing as evil being vital, but not absolute. That is to say, every man and every creature in the world is governed by the law of his own nature. As long as that person or creature is so conditioned that he can act in perfect harmony with the law of his being, his body remains in perfect health, while the whole nature works together in harmony.

As soon as any nature outside of, and adverse to, that organism, is brought into the mind, and into opposition to the workings of the law of that nature, it creates therein discord; inharmonious and adverse action, which will produce disease and, if continued, will bring death. Diseased condition means, of course, just what the word implies, a dis-eased, or an uneasy condition. The one law that I have so frequently brought before you as being the prime factor in the world, and the motive of all others to keep before the mind, i.e., use determines all qualities whether good or evil, entering into every department of existence. It forms the base of discrimination in your own mind in relation to your body, and of the services that you are to render to the world. When that law is applied in harmony with your own nature, relative to such services, all will become harmonious to you. Now, if we are enabled to carry out to a final ultimate the law of use in our own nature, we will then find that it will so harmonize our mental faculties, so open our interior, intuitive perceptions that we shall be enabled thereby to go out into the soul of nature which is the thought-world of Deity, and from the soul of nature we will, to an extent, and to a very great extent, be enabled to comprehend the mind of God in so far as it relates to all created things.

When we have reached that high pinnacle of attainment — for it is truly a high pinnacle — we can then, as from a mountain peak, overlook all the valley beneath filled, as it is, with all maimer of life, and discern in every organic form, animal and vegetable, yea, mineral, a use. Why a use? Because when we have so far harmonized our minds with the mind of the infinite so as to be able to think the thoughts of God, we then see that in that mind there is a use for everything and every condition that exists in the world.

Here is a mystery to those whose minds are not capable of making the ascension to this condition; but to those who are capable of ascending this mountain of attainment, and of finding within themselves a harmony with the infinite mind, there is no longer a mystery in what we call evil, but all becomes plain.

We thus see, as we look out into the world of animate life, that every creature that lives has its use in the world, and that use is like that of a man when he lays out a plan of a great building. When he engages in a work of this kind, he first draws the picture in his imagination of what the building is to be when completed. Then he puts that image of the brain upon paper. After he has done that, he goes to work and makes his calculations as to where all the different kinds of material are coming from, out of which this building is to be made. After he has completed these calculations, he at once employs all kinds of mechanics, from the workmen that go to the quarry, who dig down the mountain sides and blast the rocks, to the men that work with their chisels, smoothing up and squaring the stone, and those that do the finest and most delicate work in the finishing of the plans.

Now, if one inexperienced in the work of the building should come along and see all the varied workmen thus engaged, some blasting holes in the solid rock, and others polishing the stone and making it beautiful, he would look at the one with, perchance, disgust, saying, "He is tearing up and defacing the earth in thus blasting the rock." But the polishing of it up might strike him as very favorable; but this polishing could not be accomplished without the previous rough, laborious work.

So, surveying the different work, he could see how adverse one kind would be to another; how the tools which one used would be destructive to the work another was doing. Thus, if he takes the man who is blasting and puts him to work with the man who is polishing the stone, what would be the result? Why, the work would be spoiled, and in place of assisting, he would do the opposite. But when each mechanic keeps his place, works in his own department, and does his kind of work faithfully — the one mind governing all and knowing what he wants accomplished — then all work together to ultimate the one, grand purpose. Thus, we find, as we look out into nature, that every life is as busy as it can be, for life is necessarily activity; inertia is death.

Thus, we have here two principles which might be carried out so far as to say the one is evil; the other is good.

We go to the vegetable world and we there find that it is taking the elements from the earth, air, and sunlight, and carrying them up into vegetable life. Then, there are animate organisms that feed upon these vegetables. First, the insect that is the product of the decomposition of vegetable substance; then, again, there are other animals whose nature it is to feed upon those insects that are the quintessence of the plant life. Here, we see one creature eating up the other, and from the law of higher use, it is very good that this insect life should perpetuate itself. So, the work goes on, one creature feeding upon another, the higher feeding upon the lower, from the lowest grade of existence to the highest form of manhood. Every step of the way, judging from the law of the nature below, — that which is above acts as an adversary of evil, the higher laying hold upon the life of the lesser and incorporating it into their own being. Thus, the higher makes itself responsible in superior use for the life of the lower that it displaces.

Thus, we see that a world of mind is being developed through a world of matter — that in the processes of digestion; we take food into the body to nourish the mind. If you see an intellectual man, the mind is busy every day, intent on intellectual pursuits. You find it necessary to feed the body in order to supply the waste, for the food which you take into the body supplies the mind.

Now, as we look down into nature, we see there our father's workshop. All the little creatures that live are intent on gathering the chemical elements that otherwise would be wasted. They are busily engaged in gathering those elements, taking them into their organisms, preparing that chemical compound, or thought-essence, if you please, for the processes of life itself, and, in turn, we see the higher is gathering and transmuting it to something still higher, and so the line of evolutionary progress is going on from the lowest to the highest. We read that in the beginning God said, "Let US make man in our image, and let them have dominion over the fish of the sea and over the fowl of the air, and over all the earth." In this was expressed the plan of the mind of the great builder of the world, and by keeping this before us, and the question "What is the use of this and that?" we may, by the development of the intuitive faculties come to know for ourselves.

If we believe in progress, we need only to cast our eyes back a few years to find unquestionable proof of the progress of the human mind. We find there is abundant evidence that those who live now have greater capacity than any that have preceded us to find knowledge for themselves. There are two faculties in man; one is that of reason, — the other, intuition. Reason is dependent upon what it sees, hears, tastes, and smells. In short, upon the experiences, and sense-thoughts. The man who lives wholly in the material reasoning faculties, takes the plant, examines its form, and goes to his books to find out what somebody else has thought, and usually accepts it as final. If he attempts to go further, he only carries out the truth or error, as the case may be, of his predecessor; these errors are perpetuated as scientific facts; but if we call into use the intuitive and soul faculties, — known as psychometrical power, — by silencing the action of the external brain, quieting the restless struggling of the physical energies and begin to think from the great universal mind, greater and higher results are achieved. Now, what is it that is going on in such a case? As you begin to inquire, keep in mind the law of use. Go then to the plant, to the mineral, or wherever you please; place your eye upon that plant or stone. You do not know what it is. Is there in you anything that bears a likeness to the mind that made it? You all answer with one accord, "Yes!"

Yes; you are a spirit. You have a body, and you have a mind. You are a spirit. Therefore, as spirit, you may, by the alliance of the intellectual faculties to your spirit-nature, know the mind of the infinite spirit. Then silence the external mind as to the nature of the being or thing you are inquiring into, for it is only thus that you can exclude the clamor of the outer world. Then as you place your mental eye upon the object, allow the imagination to have play, and inquire into the cause and use of the thing. Then recognize as a fact that everything emanated from one source — that source being of the spirit which animates my body, and all bodies and things; for all things came from the same cause-world, and were made from the same cosmic essence. Your own spirit comes into a consciousness of the spirit essence that animates and actuates that plant as you sit silently, allowing the innermost to form its own conclusions, and to thus instruct the intellect by impressing itself on the senses. By that process you become a reader of the mind of God so that everything around you, — every plant, every animal, every stone, — will be to you a word of God, will speak to you in the language of the infinite, and tell you go about the processes which your father is carrying on in the building of that mighty temple of humanity. When the angel came to John, he showed him how it would be built out of living men and women, brought into conjunction with the infinite mind, and would stand as the king of the realms beneath. When we have reached this condition, we will comprehend the uses of what we now call evil.

Some will say, "What! Is there no adversary which is to be striven against? Are these adverse conditions that meet me in every effort to do right, not evil?" Yes; they are evil, relative to your higher and better, or real self. The flesh that you possess — the physical body, — the mind that belongs to the body — are all adverse to the spiritual, and to your efforts to ascend into a perfect consciousness of the creator. But is it evil? Let us see. We find two laws acting in all things; one emanating from God, and descending into matter; the other ascending from matter and returning to God.

Here, then, are two forces; the one, the descending currents of involution, where spirit is taking form in matter and shaping it after its own will; the other is the ultimating process of that will, which is the innermost and highest principle of nature. Then, we will call these two, the one the descending currents of involution, and the other, the ascending currents of evolution, or the spirit ascending up and working out an ultimate Son of God. How is this done? Matter has its uses in its relation to matter. Spirit has its uses in relation to spirit. Now, the spirit within you, in its uses and its relation to spirit, is that which is coming up within you into a consciousness of its kind.

God is spirit, and so are you, so far as spirit is unfolded within you. The outer mind has only a consciousness of its relations to matter, to earth, and the things of the descending currents of involution wherein spirit is bound within the limitations of material substance.

Now, as a necessity, the material mind struggles to maintain itself, to hold the charge which is committed to its care, and the animating principle that is carrying on the work of its existence. Spirit, in turn, is struggling upward to obtain consciousness of divine life. In these two processes, we find antagonism which arises from the reaction of matter. How shall we reconcile these two so that there is no longer antagonism in our nature, for in antagonism alone do we have the knowledge of sin?

We inquire into the use of this body — into the use of and workings of the spirit, for the spirit alone can give that understanding. No man, by words alone, can do so. Though I had the wisdom of an angel, and could command the intelligence of an archangel from heaven, — could even speak to you the words of God, I could never impart to you an understanding of them, save as you come into an openness and exercise of your spiritual faculties through which alone can you realize the true nature and soul of things.

Every plant, every form of life, is a perfect word of God. You must read and understand, and if you wish to understand the words of God, you must make the effort. The spirit that is like to the Creator must interpret the action of the forces which are working within. Then, in order to accomplish this ultimate and find the harmony between matter in its processes and spirit in its processes, we find that it is absolutely necessary to hold the one in abeyance, and give the ascendancy to spirit, for you cannot serve two masters. You will hold to the one and despise the other, or despise the one and hold to the other.

When you answer the question which you love the most, mind, knowledge, understanding, wisdom, which relates to God and the spirit world, or the sensuous pleasure of this body, then you are ready to decide which way you want to go. There is no standing halfway between the two.

Therein is the mystery of sin; therein is the antagonism and inharmony. How then can we find harmony in the workings of nature? The Apostle Paul said: "To be carnally minded is death, but to be spiritually minded is life" or in other words minding the things of the spirit is life and minding the things of sense is death because all that makes you a conscious entity is the thought you have of them.

If I had the power to come up before you and with a stroke of the hand drive from you, all your power to think you would be as one in a state of sleep.

When we have properly developed the spiritual consciousness, the dream state will be changed to a real consciousness of a spirit life and going to sleep will only be passing from the physical world into the spirit world. This can be obtained here and now. Then the two states of consciousness are very apparent. The consciousness of flesh is one we are all very familiar with. The consciousness of spirit is the one we all know very little about. For my part, I have chosen the consciousness of spirit because that is superior to all and from my nature I can find no happiness, no pleasure, in any other sphere of thought than that which relates to the spirit.

Now, if you feel you are decided in your own minds that you would prefer the enlargement of the knowledge which comes from the spirit of God or, if you are a member of the church and want to go to heaven, you want to be where God is. If you wish to be where God is, you must come to a consciousness of spirit. Consequently, to talk about dying and going to heaven is a fallacious hope of real life. Therefore, you must decide which it is that governs, a spiritual or a physical consciousness. If you choose the spirit consciousness, you must conquer all the desires for the gratification of the senses.

You must subjugate all the senses of the physical body, cultivating all those which arise in the spiritual consciousness, and you will discern what senses there are in the body which are harmonious and what antagonistic to your ascension into a spiritual consciousness, and as fast as you come to the knowledge of what is inharmonious, you must sacrifice it. And as you crush them out in this direction, they will awaken to a consciousness in a spiritual direction superior to that which you had before.

Thus, it is true in every sense of the word what the Nazarene said: "And every one that hath forsaken houses, or brethren, or sisters, or father, or mother, or wife, or children, or lands, for my name's sake, shall receive a hundredfold, and shall inherit everlasting life."

In coming into that spiritual consciousness, you will find that every sense which you suppress will immediately come into harmony with your ultimate work and become, as I see, a hundredfold greater and grander and more useful to your higher ideal.

Thus, by going to your inner consciousness, trying constantly to become acquainted with your real self, you will find that real self is the true man, and that the natural man is held in abeyance, for death came by sin. Life comes by the spirit, and the evolutionary process, it is said by the students of occult science, that there are men living in the world today who are several hundred years old. I have no reason to doubt it. I believe there are evidences beyond question that the power of immortality is in your own hands.

God is not an arbitrary monarch, but God is the spirit which dwells in your own soul and is ever ready to serve your own will. There is no death, no sickness, no sorrow, no pain, nothing of the kind in the spirit.

When you have brought this body into perfect harmony with that one eternal consciousness, then matter becomes as subservient to your will as it was in the beginning to your father and my father, to your God and my God. Then you will become the conscious Son of God. We are now the sons of God, but we have not awakened to a consciousness of what we are.

Now, then, the whole Question depends upon yourself. The carnal sense leads to the involvement in matter and the decomposition of the same, and when the intelligence unites with the soul from within, constantly praying, "Oh, for divine wisdom, and comprehension of the mind of God," then will you begin to realize your own inherent divinity, "A Son of God, and heir of all things."

GOD RULES
Delivered before the Society for Esoteric Culture, of Boston

We often say God rules. Probably each person that uses those words has behind them a different meaning. So diverse are the meanings and thoughts which give rise to this expression, that, could we have them all, it would take volumes to contain them. Yet one central thought is sufficient to give us the one truth in such an expression. Whilst the truth is many-sided, yet the truth is the same everywhere. The one truth has been held out to us since the history of the Christian religion, that God created the worlds by the word of his power; or that by the word of God, worlds were made. The same truth was in existence long before our Christian Bible. Away back in the dim records of the past, we find the same thought had been expressed; but with every age and every person, there is almost as great a diversity of thought as to God as there are persons.

When I say God rules, that encompasses my idea of God. For the benefit of strangers that have not heard my frequent expressions in that direction, it will be necessary to give a repetition of my thoughts. I am among those who believe that God is spirit — the all-pervading and ever-present spirit of the universe, the life giver of all things that have life, the animator of all thin that are animated. And I believe that God is not a man in the ordinary sense — that is, not limited to the confines of human form, but pervades all things. Every particle of space is filled with that Divine presence, yet that Divine presence has in it all that human intelligence can conceive of power, or thought, as to diversity of principle feeling, or emotion, and all these attributes of human existence; or, in other words, that human existence is only at the best, a faint glimmer of the Divine. Human life in its divinest ultimate can only be on earth like a dew-drop to the Sun. Like the little dew-drop that reflects the glistening light from that great luminous center, we may also, in future time, so inspire a concentrated divinity within ourselves that we may likewise shine from that Divine light. We may also be reflectors of the Divine life. Divine power, and Divine wisdom — of all the attributes of the Divine nature, that we have ever yet imagined, and many-fold more than the human brain has ever conceived.

That God created the worlds by the word of his power, comes to us from sages and seers of every class and every grade. It is a one universal truth that has illumined all minds that have received Spiritual inspiration. Then, let us consider for a moment; if God, the soul of the universe, created this little ball of ours by a word, then, all these natural laws, all these principles that produce plant life in all its diversity of forms, all the laws that unite in producing and making life in its diversified expression, yea, and the ultimate expression of human life, all these are emanations from the one mind, the one source, and the one great central, universal spirit. This being so, we find that universal Spirit is creating intelligences that are to be Spirit-like itself, having power in themselves to think, to act and to do.

According to the Hebrew Bible, God said, "Let us make man in our image, and like us, and let them have dominion over the fish of the sea and the fowl of the air, and over all the earth." To create man in the image, and like the author, creator, so that they may have dominion, power, and control of all things created, involves a process in natural unfoldment so diversified, so multifarious in its cause and effect, in its operations throughout the entire realm of nature, that the human brain, in the ordinary sphere of life, is incapable of comprehending it. That human life has evolved from a lower to a higher state of being is self-evident. In other words, there are now too many wise and powerful minds teaching the great truth of evolution from the lowest state of being up to the fulnesses of the present manhood for me this afternoon to touch that subject. It is becoming a recognized fact in the world, and it is one of the stepping-stones to a more perfect comprehension of the workings of God in nature.

When we say God rules, we have diversified ideas concerning the methods by which this is done. We may, perchance, have some methods in our minds by which we purpose to accomplish a certain result and when we fail in the accomplishment of that result, we are very apt, if we have been taught the spirit of devotion, to say: "Oh, well I God rules I" and pass it from our minds. That may be good, and it may be evil. If we recognize the fact that God rules in all the affairs of human existence, we must recognize that fact in its relation to the OBJECT in the mind of the Divine creator, as well as the method that he has at work to accomplish certain results.

Let us look for a moment into the world and see if we have reason to believe that God does rule all the affairs of life. Swedenborg well said that God could but create from himself all that there was; therefore, he must have created from himself, from the fountains of his own substance, all things, that are; so that everything that is, it but the substance of the Divinity in its varied forms and conditions. This, I know, is in opposition to what is claimed to be the Hermetic philosophy, that there were two eternal principles, matter and mind, or spirit. But if God is spirit, and God created all things from himself, then there can be nothing but spirit. Even the solids that we tread upon, the marble, the iron, the steel, and everything we know in nature, must be but a condition of spirit, a condensation of that Divine substance.

All things, then, are substance; but the relation of one substance to another may be so conditioned that two substances may be so positive and negative to each other that they may both occupy the same space at the same time without the displacement of each other. We may fill a goblet full of water; we may then fill it with a positive current of electricity; we may then fill it just as full with the negative portion of electricity, and all these will occupy the same space at the same time, myriads of other elements, or conditions of elements, may occupy the same space at the same time by virtue of diverse conditions so that the universal soul may be manifest in all the varied forms of substance, and yet be the substance of spirit, and be to us the substance of matter. All things in earth are changing; nothing stands still. Even the rock is all the time changing; the substance is being changed from one state into another. It may move slowly, but the processes of nature are certain.

We look into a world where a God spirit began the work of creation, beginning with the formation of the globe of water through generating life in the water; water animals coming forth, solidifying, and becoming ashes until the earth was formed. The earth then began to unfold its material substances and vegetation; from these came animation, and so the work of creation goes on. The life forces that are descending from the sun's rays, from the atmosphere above, and from the higher and purer essences, are all the time distilling upon our earth.

All life is living from that great substance of being, and we are inspired by that great substance and through the living organism, we create material things. Thus, true it was when God said: "Let us make man," because God works through instrumentalities. Worlds and systems existed long prior to our planet. In fact, it is believed, and we believe, that worlds and systems are as eternal as God, and that the creation of worlds and of systems is only the changing processes of the Divinity's mind, through which planets are evolved, born, grow, untold, mature, until they are fully ripened and their state etherealized until finally in the time to come this world of ours may be so refined, and so spiritualized that a world in the same plane of existence with ours will no longer be able to take cognizance of its existence. We might safely say that our planet is being carried right through the very body of immense worlds which have no consciousness of its presence. Thus, all space is filled and re-filled by orderly systems and structures that are constantly emanating from the formative Spirit, and being involved in the confines of orderly structures, and subjected to the laws of that structure for service.

Now, all this teeming life on earth is God's life, and everything that is, has life in it. When the warm sun comes in the spring, life comes forth into activity, and wherever we look we see little insects, and plant-life working out their mission on the earth. Everything seems to be teeming with life and energy; everything moves on with vigor. Yes, all his life is a part of God, the soul of the universe. Now, if I may be able to take you into the work and methods of this creation for a few moments, and make it clear to your minds, I shall be pleased; but in order to know the laws and methods of Divinity, we must seek them through the laws of our mind.

When we have given a comprehensive idea of the One Life, the One Mind, the Universal Soul that is working in and through all things, then we come to know ourselves in our own individual life, as but one form and method of the expression of the mind of Divinity in its objects and uses in the world whatever our course may have been. Whatever obstruction there may be in our pathway, we may safely say that God rules, and rules for right, by the law of His own nature. He so organizes each one of us that by virtue of our nature, and organic qualities, and peculiar construction, our mind is a photo of all we are, and when focalized, is the will, our Will, in other words, is a quintessence of all that we are. Now, let us look at that; the will is the quintessence of all that we are. We hear people say: "I can do, whatever I will to do." Yes, you can. There will be little difficulty in doing whatever the will decides you can do.

Another class has been saving for years, "God has predestined all things, and rules in all things, and therefore I can only do that which God wills me to do." That is the ultimate of the Calvinistic doctrine. These, both, are true. In this way, you had no say as to what your organic qualities should be; you are what you are by virtue of universal law without any counsel of your own will. You came into the world; you find yourself here; you find yourself possessed of certain organic qualities and of a certain will that rules you. Who made it? It is the product and expression of the universal Mind. That Mind has formed you as a word in his great vocabulary. In the language of the universe, you are a word in the great expression of his mind; and because of that, you must act out your nature. Then, some will say: "We are just what we are, and we cannot help ourselves." Let us see. There is something else. Why is it, if this be so, that you have sensations, that you are driven by circumstances to flee from one course of life to another lest you meet with accident, failure or suffering, hoping by that change you may avoid suffering? Again, you are led to conclude by the surroundings to resist and combat circumstances, and force yourself through certain lines where others are forced to give in. Perhaps you are successful, and, perhaps, you are unfortunate, and they are successful.

We know that there is a use in educating our children. We know that there is a use in developing muscle. We know that the same mind that made you, instilled life into everything, and gave the little kitten, lamb and birds, the desire to play and sport. What is the play of these little things? It is nature's gymnastics by which they develop muscles and power. The strongest and most active creatures are the most playful when young. Why? In order to be strong, they must be active. The Divine father and mother have endowed them with knowledge that is superior to that of many fathers and mothers. That child who is destined to be a very energetic man or woman is active in play. What is it active for? The divine mind rules it, and causes it to go to work and develop muscle, and provide the body with proper sinews for action. Here again is another of God's laws: By virtue of use, there is growth. That is a wonderful law when we think of it. Creation goes on by virtue of use.

Go to the surgeon and ask him, "Did you ever meet a person, who, by accident, had some great artery in the system cut off, and you tied it up so that the patient would not bleed to death, or the blood longer circulate therein? If so, what does nature do?" He will tell you, "It goes right to work and builds another canal, so that the blood goes right on." God is working not only in your body by virtue of need and use, but God is also creating mind, will, thought, intelligence, spiritual conception, and spiritual unfoldment by virtue of the use of your own quality. Use is the law that determines all qualities.

Now, then, God rules in this work of the development of mind. He rules by virtue of the organic qualities that he has projected into being, that is, as our Bible has set it forth, "That we are all members of one body," and that each of us, as members of that body, are working under the one mind, the one will, subject to the one law and the one eternal spirit. That one eternal Spirit is the animating Spirit that is controlling all our lives.

We find as we look out into the world that need and use are counterparts, and wherever there has been a need in the world, there has always been a supply. "But," says one, "we find widows and orphans suffering from hunger, dying and passing away." Has misery and suffering of the world no effect upon your mind? Is it not an instrument to develop you in sympathy and philanthropy? Does it not lay hold upon the vitals of your being and call into activity your better nature? If not, you are losing a grand opportunity, it is all working together to bring humanity up to an understanding of God's law, that we are members of one body, that no one member can suffer without all members of the body suffering, and that no part can be cut off without producing pain and suffering to others. In order to rectify the evil, we are learning this very lesson.

What is the use of experience if God rules all things? There is great use; for we read in the sayings of the prophet, "Now are we the sons of God, but it is not known what we shall be." He might as well have said we are now only children, and it is not apparent what we shall develop to be. We will, in time, be the expression of God incarnate. The work of a life-time is the work of creating knowledge, and Experience is the process that will teach us to inspire the mind potencies of the Universe; in other words, to call into existence the capacity to think about, watch for, and comprehend the works of that Infinite Soul in the world. Now, as we develop capacity, we are developing a conscious soul-life; we are individualizing our existence.

We are a part of God himself. But supposing, then, that God has all knowledge, all wisdom; we, as individual parts of the Infinite, must be individualized to an extent that we can know, and think, and be like that God; like the drop of water that it listens to and reflects the sunlight, but if we do not improve these opportunities, we will be like the drop of water that goes back into the ocean, and is as if it had not been. The object of creation is to individualize you and me, so that we may stand out as the thoughts or mind organs of the Infinite. You and I are mind-organs of the God of the universe, and the mind of the Infinite is creating organs through which He-She, the Father-Mother of all being, may express itself in the perfect harmonies of its own nature.

Now, as we look out into the world, we see two great bodies arrayed one against the other, — capital and labor, his struggle has always existed to a certain extent, and as man unfolds to a state of maturity, he is enabled to think more extensively and discriminatingly. This is beginning to take form in a fellow-feeling. It moves, and begins to unite those on the same plane of life, which causes united action in both parties. The struggle is from desire, on the one part, to get the means to live, and an effort on the other side, to subjugate the interests of the masses, and make them serve the uses of the strong.

In other words, the great cause of the straggle is the primal law of nature, by which the strongest always subsist on the weaker, and the weaker are feeling the pressure. As the masses begin to see more comprehensively the oneness of the body, they begin to rebel against that law; and the time is coming when that law must cease to dominate intelligent men. The world, up to the present, has been actuated by this common law; but we are learning, from the multifarious experiences that we have had in the past, that one part of the body cannot suffer, without all the body suffering with it. This makes the mind more universal and sympathetic, and like qualities are attracted to like qualities. Thus, we are brought face to face with antagonistic interests. Shall intelligence come to the front? Shall the spiritual nature be opened, and the blind eyes see, or must they go forward in their blindness to blood and crime, chaos and mutual destruction? It is neither desirable nor necessary that they should go to that point.

If we awaken to the fact that God is spirit, that we are all members of one body, and that each is a member in particular, and that one cannot suffer without all suffer; then we will begin to recognize that we are all interested in one common result. Then, instead of the stronger subsisting on the weaker, the strongest will begin to use their powers to lift up the weaker. The strongest men are the wealthiest men; for it is through strength they obtained the wealth; for business is a combat in which the strongest prevails. This law marks a fact in nature: that the working man is the weakest in this business combat.

What is it that is of value that God is working through man to ultimate? What is most valuable in man? The mind that is strongest, the mind that is best adapted to that Divine expression. That is the man who is most fully unfolded, and is truly rich. The great wisdom of Divinity is manifest in such a variety of ways that we, when we once comprehend it, can reach that point of knowledge, that God rules, and we need be anxious for nothing.

By looking out into the world, and analyzing carefully the mental phenomena that governs the man, that accumulates wealth and keeps it, you will find that he invariably, in his private life and methods of reasoning, can be called a very superstitious man. That man is governed by his dreams, or by his peculiar feelings, or impulses, or by the first thought that comes to his mind, or by some law or sign that he has adopted, and he lets that be the law that governs him; and as that comes from the superior power, by virtue of its being accepted as his law, he is made a steward of the Divine mind to control the wealth of the world. The men that are ruling, and the holders of the wealth of the world, have a consciousness that they are but the stewards of the Almighty.

There are but few men on this planet to-day but what, if some demand should be made on them, that was in perfect accord with their law, for half they possess, would give it. Now we find that this law that rules the world is a just law; and that if every one of us can be satisfied to move forward, watching carefully all the indications from the soul, — for, mark you, I repeat that the men who make the money and keep it, are the men that are governed by the moving of the soul, — and are faithful to that law, we shall be made such stewards according to our desires.

You have a use in the world. What that use is you can never know by any other method than by first finding what the law of your being is. Your attention has been called to the fact that we must find out the dominant principle of our nature. The dominant principle, or key-note, of our nature is what determines the law of rights to us. The man that is most intuitive is the successful man. He has been made most conscious of that key-note, and has been faithful in following and obeying its laws.

There are two minds. One is the solar; the other, the astral. The animals are led by the solar mind; the instincts of the birds, beasts, and all things, are governed by that mind. As soon as they are born, they know what kind of food is their natural prey; each knows just where and how to protect itself. There is another mind referred to, which we call the astral, or spiritual mind, — the mind of the spiritual man; it is contrary to the mind of the animal man. In looking into the "solar man" of the zodiac, we find that our earth passes through the solar forces from head to foot. All the animals and men in pursuit of physical wealth are controlled by that mind, and are working together to carry forward the work of creation in the world; to carry on, make and keep conditions suitable to gratify that mind. The spirit of God in creation may descend into matter, and find expression in physical structure. That is the work of the planetary force of our system. The other is the work of evolution, drawing the mind from the intellectual up to the spiritual, and through that, to the consciousness of God.

The sun is but another world revolving round another sun, and the sun is revolving in the reverse direction to the planets of our system, from the feet towards the head. Thus, in the higher realm of life, there is a direct antagonism between the two orders; also, between the two processes of mind. The minds that follow the animal instincts, and have strong physical bodies, succeed through the strength of the body and mind. But the man who is more allied to the spiritual and intellectual does not succeed in the business world, because his mind, sympathies, and powers are divided. He is trying to live in two worlds, but is not fully adapted to either. To be a successful man, he must give all his powers to one or the other.

God rules and is the Supreme Good. He rules in creation, and in the world of matter, and the man that values the intuitions and the law that he has made is successful. This is the law of regeneration. The man who follows the spirit is the man that is apt to be left m want for a time. But when, through regeneration, he begins to be consciously one with the Father, then the universal will that rules his organism, and all the affairs of the earth is one; and he, by means of the same ruling will that was the dominator over these men, causes that which is now antagonistic, in this lower sphere, to work together not only for his good but for the good of all those who are coming up out of this animal into the spiritual condition.

The time has come, when, in my opinion, there must be a reconstruction in the governing power of men and women, that their spiritual consciousness becomes one with God's consciousness, who now looks down upon the workings of the world with charity and love. So will man and woman, when they have come to a spiritual consciousness, overlook everything in the world, and by that interior mind, the "still, small voice," they will rule the affairs of the earth. Then and not till then will this take place.

When there are a number of such human instruments that have ultimated these higher attainments so that God's mind can find perfect expression through their organism, then God's will, that rules all things, will also find perfect expression through them; and they, having come into order and harmony with the Divine law, God will, through them, bring order out of disorder and harmony out of chaos. Let it be one, two, three, four, or a hundred and forty-four thousand — the number given to John at Patmos, that "would be the first ripe fruit of the earth." — Ripe fruit implies growth, development, unfoldment and maturity.

God rules your mind according to the ultimates of your being. All these things are working together to make you the expresser of God's law, which may be briefly stated thus: we are individual members of one grand body and, as individuals, we must perfect our individuality. In doing this, we come to a consciousness of our oneness with God as the animating Spirit of all, and we shall then see the necessity of the body being together as one body, and all separateness will cease. There will be one God, one soul, one body, one purpose, one power ruling and overruling all; then the "Kingdoms of this world will become the Kingdom of God and of his Christ," i.e., his anointed body. Peace be with you.

I KNOW I KNOW
Delivered before the Society Esoteric of Boston

We have often heard the words which usually are brought out in controversy, "I know I know that such is the case! I know, I know it!" Now there is a question here. The question seems to be; "From what standpoint do we know?" We see, and from the sense of sight, we know. We hear, feel, taste, or we touch, and from that we decide we know. May you not as well say, "I know that in my dream last night such-and-such a thing occurred?" was not that dream as real as some experiences that you have had in a normal state of the physical body?

I presume we have all had dreams that were impressed as deeply and strongly upon our consciousness as any experiences in our life, all the senses participating in the dream. Now the question arises, was it real, or was it a hallucination? The question has been discussed in the philosophical ranks and among the students of occult sciences in all their branches, as to what this consciousness is that in the dream-state appears to us like knowledge. Again, there is another point to be discussed in this question, as to "what are the sources from which to obtain real knowledge."

This latter subject is one that seems to be most directly related to our everyday life. We are engaged in the different pursuits of life, and we are gaining experiences thereby, and those experiences form the base and, to a large extent, the scope of the knowledge of the nineteenth century. Should we not ask the question, "what reality is there in all these physical experiences?" This question might be answered only by the aged.

You ask the aged man that has seen sixty, seventy or eighty years in the same neighborhood: "What were the conditions and surroundings of this place in your boyhood days?" After he has given you a complete analysis or picture of the surroundings in his youth, you look around you and find scarcely any of those conditions now. All seem to have passed away, and been replaced by new ones. Those experiences in their time were real, but they were transient. They were real to the physical senses, but they were soon to pass away.

We have, all of us that have in any way looked into spiritual subjects, thought about the world to come. We have thought that at some time, when we had finished the experiences of this life, we should enter an eternal world, an existence that would continue throughout the endless ages. But all that arises from the state of our personality, individuality, or personal consciousness, and that consciousness is made up of the experiences of this life, that is our education. If we should forget all that we have ever learned, there would be no difference between us — intellectually — and a child just born. After forgetting all that was past, all that related us to a personal consciousness would be lost, leaving us only the life and physical body which would enable us to go on and experiment in the affairs of life and obtain knowledge concerning things that are here, but that knowledge would be like the things from which it was derived.

Now, that being so, where is the immortality of the soul whose existence is wholly made up of the experiences of a transient life?

But supposing we ask the man who lived fifty years ago upon the site where Chicago now stands, "What was there then?" Very little. Ask him to go there today and is there anything that he recognizes? No. All the experiences that he then had only to remain in memory, the real has passed away.

Again, let us suppose the possibility of the man who lived fifty years ago in Chicago, lying down and going to sleep. He slept soundly during these fifty years, at the end of which time he awakens and looks round to find his home. All is changed. Had he forgotten the experience prior to that sleep, he would then be like a child just born, having to learn all about the things of the world. But what would be the nature of the memory of such a one? would it not be identical with that of a dream? Certainly it would; for there would be nothing to link the consciousness of the present with the memories of the past, therefore it would seem unreal. There are many in the world now who have such memories of a prior existence in the earth, but if they were never able to link the two states together, it would never become a conscious reality. The soul being made by the spirit out of the substance and life of the body, when the soul has neither spirit nor body, it has nothing out of which to build new experiences and the old would pass away by the changefulness of everything earthly. And as the vitality, with which it was endowed by the body, would gradually fade away like the memory of an aged man who forgets everything — even his own children — as the vitality of the body departs, so his consciousness dies before the body and, in some cases, afterwards.

We are so peculiarly constructed in our organic life, that the senses form to us a continual consciousness; for it is only the senses that perpetuate our consciousness, and as the senses primarily belong to the physical body, the question now arises, "Is it possible for the senses to pass away?"

We have often heard men say. "I will not believe anything that I cannot comprehend, that does not come within the scope of my five senses." This position is quite prevalent; the teachings of the last two hundred years have predominated in this line of thought. But when we lay off this body, it returns to its earth, and this class of minds must die with the body, or soon after. It is the thinking principle of intelligence, at such times, that is active during the night, when the body is in a dead sleep, which constitutes all that remains of the man's consciousness and acts.

If you stop, and carefully analyze it and experiment on its phenomena, you will find that, if you lie down and get into a perfectly passive state in which the mind leaves the realm of the senses, your mind is intently musing on some occurrence of life or something that you have idealized as a subject or thing that you wish to bring into existence. You pass into that subjective state, or into that thought world, so that your whole mind is lost in the musings upon that subject. You will observe, as you pass out of the physical consciousness, that you pass into a realistic condition concerning the subject you were thinking about, and the more fully developed the soul life is, the more real will those ideas and images stand out that you had formed in your mind whilst musing upon such subjects. If, perchance, you have had in mind that in some future time, perhaps years hence, you would go to some locality where there was a prospect that a city would be reared, and if you had contemplated going there to lay the foundation and begin the mechanical work necessary to establish that city, even though you had placed the event far hence to enable you to collect means by which to accomplish it, yet in this attitude you would think how the progress of that city would take place, about the form of the buildings that would be reared, the streets, and the relation that one would bear to the other. You thus go on, as you pass into that subjective state, imagining the thing that is not yet in existence, you would observe then that prospective city would become to you a real city. You might, as you pass into dream-states, your mind being all absorbed upon that subject, find yourself in the streets of that city, enjoying subjectively the benefits of your labors of the years yet to come. By what consciousness would all this become real to you? By this subjective process of mind. Now, right here, you get a little idea of what the soul's consciousness is, independent of the physical body. If, while your mind was absorbed in this direction, and during the time of your thought's intensity in imagining such a subject, you should sit down and write a letter to a friend, and that friend, being very sensitive, had developed the powers now known as psychometry; as soon as he took that letter and held it passively in the hand, or on the forehead, he, or she, perchance, might see your image, and in connection with it the images that you had created in your mind concerning the said city would stand forth in the imagery of his or her mind. These imaging's would be perceived as if they really existed, and there are those who might go to such minutiae as to tell all about it and where such an ideal city was, or was to be. "What does this argue?" The writer held that letter in his hand, and an animal magnetism, the subtle energies of his life, has entered into the paper, and the senses of the psychometrist have discovered what the emanations of his life were, and with what thoughts the letter is impregnated. Now from that we can go a little further back.

If the emanations of the physical body will impregnate a piece of paper with such imaginings, feelings, and emotions, then certainly all these imaginings, feelings, and emotions have formed a part of the structure of the physical body. They have given quality to the physical body. Then, if they have riven it quality, you can readily see that they will give color to all the senses, according to their quality. Now, there are persons who will partake of articles of food that to us are very repugnant; perhaps we could not digest them at all. Yet they eat such articles of food and delight in them. Why so? Because their senses are quite different from ours. Now all thought arises in sense, and you take a person and let him think about an article of food and you think about the same, and see what a wide diversity there will be in the thoughts concerning it, and in the sensations, it will produce in the two.

Now just as wide a divergency as exists in the senses of the persons would be the breadth of divergency in the consciousness of individuals. So that if we take five, six, ten, twelve, or twenty persons, and let a musician sit down and run over the keys of a piano or organ, and let each one observe carefully which one of those sounds was most harmonious to him, we would find a great diversity of opinion as to which were the sweetest and most melodious. The same divergency exists in regard to amusements, or would exist, if persons going to the theatre were in the habit of thinking independently; but unfortunately, we have been in the habit of taking what somebody else has said as to whether a thing was good or bad, and are governed by what the majority say. How many times we have gone to places of amusement, or heard music of some famed musicians, and because they were famed, the audience generally pronounced the performance grand, and they thought it grand, but let some unknown persons play the same, even execute it in a far superior manner, and the same audience would say it did not amount to anything. This is from the habit that exists among people of being led by the majority; yet among the independent thinkers themselves, there would be a diversity of opinion corresponding to the difference in their natures, so that what you think you know, and what another thinks he knows, would be so different as to antagonize if not destroy each other.

Now we advise you, as the stepping-stones to a self-consciousness and to an independent thought, and the building of your own soul's existence, to begin to watch those little things. In regard to this matter of music, you go there, and if among all the persons that are independent in their thought, and look to the play or music for the personal pleasure they find in it, one would choose certain parts that others would reject. This is only a further proof of the fact that, whilst you say "I know that such-and-such conditions exist from all my senses," another person, under the same circumstances, would say with the same emphasis, "I know that such-and-such conditions do not exist." Both are equally honest in their judgment and decision.

Now, here is where we are brought to consider, first, of all things in life, our own personal consciousness; and in the consideration of this thought, you will find greater advantage in making the attainments, or in your efforts to climb the heights of knowledge, than in other directions. By this method, only can you find out your own real nature. Your thoughts, senses, conclusions, etc., are being controlled by public opinion. When you say, "you know," from what do you know? From these senses. The senses are just what your consciousness at the time has made them. For instance, were you sitting quietly with your hand down by your side, and it was very cold weather and someone would touch your hand suddenly with a very hot piece of iron; if it did not remain there long, you would decide that it was a piece of ice, especially if your mind happened to be on the experiences of the cold; on the other hand, you might be touched with a piece of ice and be confident that it was a heated iron. Such is the disposition of our senses. What, and where is the real?

We are living here in a business world, where the whole mind of each one is being concentrated on one line of thought and action in order to succeed. Circumstances are such in this combat, — this battle-field of existence in which we live, — that they force every man and every woman, who has not treasure laid up sufficient for independent living, to concentrate all their powers of thought, which is their consciousness, into the efforts of self-preservation. Since this is so, what can we know about Eternity. What can we know about the causes when our whole mind throughout a life-time is absorbed in the physical senses of a business world, having developed nothing but a consciousness of the animal senses and powers? We return to earth as babes, such as we were when we first came, so far as any unfoldment is concerned. Could we as babes enjoy the world as fully as a more mature man? We think not. Why? Because the capacity for enjoyment is the measure of the capacity of your intellect, of your thought, of your consciousness. There are persons that are incapable of suffering one half as much as other persons under the same circumstances, because they are not so finely organized; they are not so intelligent, and there is not as much life in the body, neither is the life as fine and sensitive.

Some of you have observed when you started out for a carriage ride, and with a fresh, spirited horse, that, when you first started out, you dared not raise the whip. You drove on and on, and as night approached, the horse began to lose his energy, and you would begin to urge him. At first, he would start up briskly when the whip was applied, but the next time, less so. When the life had been thrown off with which the body was filled at the time of starting out, then you might strike him with the whip, and he would not flinch. Why is this? That horse having thrown off the life-essences does not feel the same as he did. With the life went his capacity to feel suffering.

In my own experiences while I was in the army, marching day and night, so exhausted was my vitality that I was incapable of suffering. My body merely moved as a machine; there was no sensation left; that had passed away from me. I then went through that which, under other circumstances, would have caused intense suffering. What does this tell us? That I had exhausted the life essences and so lessened my conscious perception. The life is the cause by which we move, and as we waste it, the body loses its energy, and as it ebbs away, the mind loses its consciousness. Those persons who have the highest and most intense refinement of life in their organisms are the persons who suffer the most intensely. This is no new thought. Take any proficient student of human nature, a phrenologist if you please, whose business it is to judge of the intellectual abilities of men and women, and it will be found they all understand this if they really understand their business. They will say to this one, "you suffer intensely and enjoy intensely;" to another, "you can go through a great deal and not flinch." The latter feels flattered, but he is on a lower plane of life; he is more in the animal body; he has less power of feeling in his nature; he cannot appreciate the things that the other appreciates, neither can he think the thoughts the other one thinks, because the qualities are not there.

Therefore, before any of us can enjoy our ideal heaven, we have got to make conditions, in order that it may be a heaven for us, as our future existence will be just what we have made ourselves.

We return a moment to the imagination of the man that built the ideal city. That ideal city was just as real to him as if it had already been built. This consciousness that was active in his dreams is the consciousness that is active in the man or woman after the body has returned to dust.

Then, these things being so, it is obvious that the imaginings of your mind are the creative factors on the cause side of life. This agrees exactly with the Hebrew Bible, and, in fact, with all the ancient religions where they unite in saying, "By the word of God, the worlds were made." All things were created by the word of God. What is a word? You, through this process of thinking, formed an ideal in your mind. After you have the ideal formed, you speak the word; you give out that ideal; it is gone from you. You may forget it; forgetting it is merely the loss of ability to call it back again. That word has cost some of your life-energy. You have taken the sublimated essences of your life which you get through the processes of your physical body, by taking nourishment, sunlight, and electric currents from the earth, all of which have united in feeding the body. We know that a man that is thinking intensely has to feed the body accordingly. The action of thinking is the act of taking the sublimated essences that are generated through the processes of the body, forming them into thoughts, and giving them out. These same processes of taking the life-essences of our own body, forming images, and sending them out, were the processes by which the God of the universe created worlds. This is the united conclusion of all the masters, down to the present time. All philosophers agree with this.

This imaging process that you possess, is the likeness that you bear to the divine creator, and every thought that you image in your mind, is as real as any substance, and in fact, thoughts are the only real things remaining when we lay off this physical body. They are the only things there are, no others are real after that time. You try an experiment. You go to a trance medium, and he, or she, goes into that trance state in which the body is entirely unconscious; they have passed into the dream state. The soul is conscious, it perceives; it sees beside you such-and-such a person, perhaps describing them minutely, and you may recognize them. What does it see? It does not see the physical body at all; it sees with those eyes that look at the soul of things. The medium may describe the dress of the friend that is seen beside you, which was a dress worn many years ago by that person. You may go into a house or room, where some person has lived for years, whose mind scarcely ever went beyond the sphere of his home. He lived and grew in the house. You, if you have developed the soul-sight, may see him after the body dies and is laid away; you would see the form of the person the same as in life; you would see the returned soul of the person, but it can only be seen in this subjective state, and, when in this state, the person appears just as real, just as tangible, as he was in life. Thus, when you pass into the subjective state, you see that which is in the subjective. You see your own soul and other souls that may be the joint possessors of your body with yourself. It is no new idea that the body is occupied by more than one soul. We read that the Nazarene cast a demon out of a single body. Out of Mary Magdalene, he cast seven demons before she could become a fit disciple. If we should pass into that state, and survey this temple of the body, we might, all of us, find that we were possessed by more than one demon.

That is the spirit world, known to spirit mediums; it is the subjective world, which is the border-land between the real world, from which the physical world came, and this physical world is the outgrowth of the subjective one, of which we speak.

Now let us inquire, "What do we really know?" that is, those of us who are engaged wholly with this physical and external world. We perceive readily that we can know nothing but this shadow-world which is rapidly passing away. We cannot even know the essential elements and essences and causes, that actuate our own physical body. We are living, like the brute creation in the physical senses, and know nothing beyond them; we are like a thing that is acted upon by a superior, and that superior one we know nothing about. As we have shown, we think conclusively, that the physical senses are extremely deceptive: therefore, what you know in the physical senses is not knowledge at all.

Out of an idea, you may become a creator, and give the idea tendencies towards coming into the objective. For instance, if you should spend your life, or a portion of it, in the conception of some mechanical device which was going to be of great value to the world, and kept it secret in your own mind, treasured it closely, and dwelt upon it constantly, but never attempted to put it into form, the first thing you would know, someone else would catch the idea, and give it a physical form, even though you had never told anyone about it. Their sensitive mind called it in, went to work, and worked it out. Thus, we are constantly creators, being made in the image and likeness of God.

All these senses that belong to the physical body unite, as the hands, to carry out the image work of the more perfect man, to bring it into physical form. You, who are living wholly in the phenomena of the five senses, know nothing of this factor, this Creator behind the physical senses. You only know the thing produced. An animal may become conscious of the presence of a thing, as well as we, but it cannot become conscious of the Mind that has the capacity to create. It takes the higher minds for that. Therefore, the first step should be to develop these inner powers by experimenting upon the effects of thoughts that arise in your mind, and the feelings that course through your body; for these ideals that flit through the like mind, may be the creation of another mind. Therefore, when we begin to study self, to understand the laws and methods of this body, and begin to try to go beyond the physical senses, we are then just beginning to get where we can say "I know I know I" and not before. When we come to where we can, of a truth, say, "I know that I have a consciousness of something that is beyond, that is superior to, and therefore controls, the physical organism and the physical world," — that is the beginning of knowledge, but it is only the first step in the ladder. There are yet many steps beyond this. There is a cause beyond every effect, and we are now in a world of effects. We are here to begin the trial of becoming like the Creator, to begin with the world of effects, which are related to the physical senses, going interior, and tracing the effect from cause to cause, and so back towards the prime mover of all things. Thus, we have an endless road to travel, and the further we go on that road, the broader, the grander, the more perfect, will be the consciousness and the power within, to say "I know I know I."

THE MIND OF WISDOM
Delivered before the Society of Esoteric of Boston

Where should we go to find the mind of wisdom? Should we go far away from our planet? Should we soar into the spheres? Should we go to some far-off world to find the manifestation of wisdom? Or can we but awaken, look around us on every side into the wondrous workings of Mother Nature, and find there the mind of wisdom? I say could we but awaken! For it is true, and more fully so than many of us are aware, that we, with the whole world of animate life, are sleeping, and have been so for ages. Here and there one is awaking a little from his slumber, like one that is disturbed in the sleep of the night, and vaguely asking himself, "What is it? Where am I?" And as we thus awake to a more complete consciousness of existence and look around us and inquire, "What is life? What am I here for? What are the uses I am supposed to serve in this physical existence? What relatedness do I bear to all the rest of the universe? And how shall I best utilize my time? Again, what relatedness is there between my conscious self and the Infinite Mind?" These are questions that will open the door to the fountain of knowledge and true wisdom. We need not go into the sphere of worlds beyond us, or the labyrinth of space, to find an expression of wisdom. We need to turn our attention only to this planet of ours.

In the spring-time we see our planet bring forth life of every form and character. The whole planet is teeming with life, from the smallest microscopic insect to the highest order of manhood, all partaking of the one animating principle; all born from the one mother, from the same life-emanations, governed by the same unknown mind that is acting in and through us, and which find expression in the same as in the vegetables below us, causing manifestations of life through our own physical bodies of which our intellect has no knowledge nor power of control. We are as a vegetable, growing in a world where there is a power that propels us forward. We move on and say: "This is the law of necessity, the law of life," recognizing, in a word, that there is a law, yet not cognizant of its methods, a law that has order, method, formula. All that pertains to the law of intellectuality we find expressed in the physical universe, in everything that lives, and wherever we turn our attention, we can but conclude that the mind thus working in all existence has a definite object in view, an ultimate toward which all this busy, active energy of life is laboring. Is there not a well-defined object in this Superior Mind that has brought us into being, and brought all nature into existence, that controls and environs us by circumstances that we cannot resist, impels us forward? For what object? This is a question for the mind to answer. The mind alone that has wisdom can penetrate to this realm, the only realm of thought that relates in any way to the important uses, not alone of the present but of the time to come. If there is any question worthy of a religious consideration, it is this subject and these laws, and the object in the mind of this creative power, that is pushing us forward. May we not know what that object is?

There are multitudes of beliefs in the world concerning the law of God, and many judge of God as of an earthly monarch, whose laws are mere edicts; but to my mind it seems that the whole subject resolves itself down to a very simple problem. There are but few in our world today but what accept as a fact that there is superior intelligence that has projected into being all things that are. (With the few who do not accept this, and claim that all the potencies of creative mind are in matter, we, perchance, were it not for lack of time to explain, could likewise agree, and also with those who believe in a superior and infinite intelligence, and show that we all believe the same thing). But to believe in a mind that governs the universe, is to believe that all that is in the world is there because of that mind. If there is a creator of all things, all things having been created from that one fountain, then we cannot avoid the conclusion that all things are by and because of this will as the Nazarene so well said: "You cannot by taking thought make one hair white or black." That is, you cannot by mere thought, change any of the conditions of your life. We are what we are. We find ourselves here; we find ourselves in the present environment. Now all that is left for us is to look around, and find out where we are and what there is for us to do; and what we are as well and after we have answered the question, "What am I?" then we can go further, and look out into the universe, and find this I, this ego, this self, magnified millions of times. As we turn our attention to Nature, we find that everything that is in this world is in our bodies, and everything that is in the body is in the world. And in answer to this question, "What am I?" we say, "I am the universe epitomized."

The majority of humanity has never thought beyond the five senses. We have lived in the five senses until it is a common expression, and more common thought, that "I am this body, and this physical body is myself," simply because through this body, through the senses of the physical comes all our consciousness; therefore, we have been in the habit of thinking of ourselves as merely of earth. But let us consider death?

Think what a change comes over the person who at one moment was full of life and animation, but through some accident, the life has departed — the body is dead! Why is this change that transpires in the organism? What is the cause of it? The lips are pale; the eyes lose their expression, and everything is changed radically. The man is not there; he no more senses, no longer thinks; no longer has the power of action. The essential, the real, the thinking, the intellectual, conscious ego is not there. The body alone is there. Then, I am not a mere material, physical body. I am something that is more subtle than the matter that we handle, taste, and see. The natural eye does not see mind. The I that thinks, the I that feels, the I that has consciousness, the I that has volition, is not the physical, but the ethereal or spiritual.

Again, we see the corn and the grass grow. Can we see the potential energy that causes it? We may watch week after week the growing corn, or grass, or vegetable. We see that they do grow; but we do not see the life-energy which, causes it. Growth is the process of materializing the ideas of the universal mind, for we cannot comprehend or believe the idea of something having expression out of nothing. We may force the brain to accept it, but can we, in our innermost self, believe it? No; it is contrary to the highest intelligence of our nature. We may force ourselves to believe, but, down deep, there is something that says, "No; it cannot be. No; this something that I am, enables me to think for myself and control in certain lines of thought, it is governed by certain laws, it is limited by certain desires, and that something must be, yes, is derived, from this one great Mind, whose workings find expression in all forms of life. For they all spring into existence by the same law, are nourished by the same life-emanations, and are, necessarily, all members of one body.

But are we here merely to be dragged along without mind or volition through this checkered life, and then lie down and be as if we had not been? "No," says one, "we are here to do the best we can through this life, and then die and go to heaven, somewhere beyond the bounds of time and space, where we will be happy forever." To a heaven? Has God a storehouse somewhere, where all his creatures of the untold millions of worlds are gathered in one place? What would there be in that? We find, as we look abroad in nature, everywhere, that the law of being is the law of use; do we not find that in every-day life, in our own experiences, that use determines all qualities, whether good or evil? It certainly does. You cannot determine what is good or evil by any other principle. If you should see a man going along the street bearing a heavy burden upon his shoulders, and you knew that burden, perchance, has a lot of old papers that had long since ceased to be of any value, and yet he was lugging them around all the time, you would say: "What is the use in that man bearing that burden? What a fool he is! He must be insane." Why? Because it is of no use to him. The law of use is the law of being. Then the question comes home to you: What is the use of your present existence, of your advent here upon this earth? You were born for true manhood and womanhood. You now see the world opening before you. What is it for? Is it merely to struggle to get a livelihood for threescore years, and then after that pass away and enter into a heaven, a paradise that you have not earned, where you cease to be of any use but merely to have enjoyment? Would there be enjoyment in it? I think not; such a condition would be that of misery instead of enjoyment. No man or woman can find pleasure in anything but usefulness: it is contrary to the law of life to be useless, and the man or woman that ceases to be useful ceases to be happy. We might as well think of being happy in the theological hell, as to expect to be happy in leading a useless life. Then, if this law of use is the dominant law of being — which we see very readily it is — then what is the use of this world teeming with life in every form? What is the use of such diligence being manifested in every form of existence?

See the Insects, how busy they are! They spring forth into existence, they at once begin to labor. We see them as busy as they can be from the early morning until the night sets in; and sometimes it seems as if they would labor night and day, gathering food for the body. What IS the use of this? Through the processes of that body, they transmute and transform their food into germs of new existences through which multitudes of other lives spring forth. And their whole labor is to gather the fallen elements and incorporate them in their own structure; and then yet higher creatures are equally active, gathering up those same insects, incorporating them in turn, organizing this insect-life into higher structures. Every creature has its "natural adversary," another animal to whom it is a natural prey. The lower is the natural prey and food of that above it. Thus, in the life that springs into existence in the early spring, from the earth, yes, in the waters of the ocean; there is a regular line of one creature feeding upon another, from the lowest conceivable form, all the way up to man; for man, like other animals, is feeding on, and incorporating the life of the animals below him. So, there is an unbroken chain, in the ascending currents of life, from the very lowest to the highest. What for? What is the use of all this? Can there be an expression found that will answer better than the one in Genesis, chap, i, verse 26. "And God said: Let us make man in our image and like us, and let them dominate over the fish of the sea, the fowl of the air, and every living thing upon the earth." The Hebrew form of expression where it says: "Let us make man in our own image" is identical with the expression that occurs after, where we are told that Eve bore a son in her own image; the word image and the word son in that place are synonymous. You will see the same idea is correctly shown in John's Gospel where he said: "In the beginning was the word, and the word was with God, and the word was God."

We will repeat for the benefit of those not present when we gave our explanation, a short time since, of what constitutes a "word." We take food into the body to nourish it as passes through all the chemical changes until it finally becomes a sublimated essence, and is called up to the brain, where it is formulated into thought and sent out into the world by the will, and with that thought as it is formed in us and sent out, goes a part of our life. The man or woman who is busy in thinking is necessitated to feed the body in proportion as much as the man or woman that labors hard with the muscles. The sensitive can go into a room where words have been spoken, collect their essence in his brain, and give them out again, which proves that thoughts are things. In the beginning was the word that went forth into nature, and that word, John said, was God, i.e., "Power," for the word "God" means "Power," and the word had power in itself to create. "All things were made by Him; and without Him was not anything made that was made. In Him was life; and the light was the life of men;" and then he refers to the manifestation of the Son of God, Jesus, who was the most perfect man that ever walked our planet earth, being the expression of the Word of creative energy, and the image of the ultimate towards which all creation labors. Yet Jesus indicated that his work was not the perfect and final ultimate, for he said: "Greater things than these shall ye do." But as we have not done them, we must conclude that they are yet to be worked out. The central thought in the beginning that formed our life, and of which this teeming world of life is the emanation, from whose energy all animate life is laboring so diligently, and toward which we are working is, to bring into manifest existence a spiritual manhood and womanhood which shall be in all their feelings and emotions like the thought from which the world originally came.

What is our life? Some two or three times every day, we have to feed this body. We have, again, to get material to clothe it and keep it warm. How busy we are! We are made to labor because of this, our ward tide. Onward to what? Or is it not time for us to consider the question? Toward what are we going? For what are we here? Ask nature. We need not ascend into heaven to ask a God, nor descend into hell to ask a Devil. No! As the apostle Paul has well said: "The word is nigh thee in thy hearty that infinite word, the word of wisdom, the word of knowledge, the word of understanding, the power to comprehend the universe within you; and it is your RIGHT to come into a consciousness of God and His work, for you are the Son of God; you are a creator. How do we know? Physiology tells us that these bodies of ours that we have to-day, will, within the limits of seven years at least, be gone, and a new one built. Can you do such a work as that? Could you, in seven years' time, take a body all to pieces and build a new one, keeping the same vital energies active in it? Is there a scientist in the world that has the mind of wisdom to do it? So, all that there is for us to do is to know ourselves and the mind that is within us. Think of the ability of that wonderful chemist to take that mass of material that you are putting into your stomach, and from it to make a chemical analysis, taking out the necessary qualities for the body, and throwing off all the rest; taking out that which is food and rejecting the unfit, for the purpose of rebuilding this body. This wonder of wonders, this wise chemist, is in you, and it is within your power to cultivate that mind, to bring it into the intellect, that you may know, that you may comprehend it with all its power, all its methods; that all its keen, discriminative ability may be known and understood fully by your intellectual self!"

In consideration of this fact, are we not asleep?

What knowledge are we acquiring? Simply what somebody else has taught us about what someone else has known; nothing of our own interior consciousness! And what do our physiologists know of our real nature? They know the form of the brain, muscles, etc., but of course they know nothing. But, Oh, that mind of wisdom that you are! If you can only come to the one consciousness, "I am not the flesh; I am superior to flesh, and what I have learned through these physical senses is only the mechanical structure, — the phenomena of an inner workman, of whom we know nothing," and yet: that workman is ourselves. All that work which appears is only a shadow, here to-day and gone tomorrow; of the mighty intelligence that built the structure, we have no knowledge.

Where is the mind that has wisdom? Look within your own soul, counsel the Muse, the Guide! Examine the thoughts that frequently spring up within yourself, that inform you of things which your reason has no capacity of knowing! We find they tell us grand truths, and often save our life when danger is unforeseen to the intellect. It is the voice of God that we as men and women have closed our ears to during the centuries past, and therefore know nothing of it. The time was, in the golden age of the world, when men were governed from within, by that mind, and were in God's Eden.

We have, through a long period of experiment, acquired great brain power, and are a humanity highly developed in the intellect, and greatly degenerated in the animal faculties, but endowed with a brain structure that is capable through mechanical device to harness the elements and make them our servants. Now, when we consider what the human intellect has been able to achieve from its reasoning abilities: what power, what knowledge, what understanding, what wisdom would this brain be capable of if united with the God that animates this body? This Mind should be our guide in everything we do, for It has wisdom.

The Bible deals with man as a trinity, whilst the Orientals teach a seven-fold combination of man. The trinity is easier to grasp, and comes more directly to our comprehension. We are then, body, soul, and spirit. The spirit is the cause; the soul is the reasoning, intellectual entity, whilst the body is animated animal existence. God is spirit, who is from eternity, and His word is in you, and says to you now the same as in the beginning, "Let us make man in our own image, and like us, and let them (spirit, soul and body,) have dominion over all the earth." By the contact of spirit with the physical body (matter), and through the experimental life in which we live, we have organized a soul. This soul, the reasoning intellect, is counseled by the Spirit of God as if it were a king, and whatever decision is made by this soul, the intellect, which is the Son of God: The God within serves obediently to carry it out. It will not guide you in that which is contrary to your real nature, but it will give you the power to act, experience, and reap the full reward of your own deeds.

Surely, the spirit of wisdom is active within you. Should your intellect decide that you are ready to give your life to co-work with God, it will teach you all things and reveal things to come, for it knows the future as the present, and has access to all power in heaven and on earth. This interior is your father, your creator, and the real self. It is eternal. Everything not of it must be dissolved and pass away. Therefore, to have eternal life, we must have a soul (intelligence) in unity with it, or it will leave us at the death of the body, and then we must dissolve, or re-incarnate and finish that which was neglected, the "at-onement."

Now, we have come to a time when we are able, some of us at least, to grasp God the Mighty Soul of the Universe, and if we will turn our attention to be a co-worker with Him, He will co-work with us. "All that the Father knows," as Jesus said, "He will show it unto us," and we shall know the Mind of God, as we now know our own mind, and therein possess the mind of Wisdom.

UNITY OF DESIRE

All can agree with this; that God, — or the Son of the Universe and Author of all Being, is One; that all beneficent qualities flow from that One; and that the vital principle in all religions is harmony with, and submission to, the Will, or "Laws" of that one Spirit.

Now, can we not all unite our prayers as one man on these words and the thoughts they express: "Our Father who art in heaven, hallowed be Thy name. Let Thy kingdom come. Let Thy will be done on earth, as it is in heaven." —

Let us analyze these words and find what they really contain?

It is a habit of children to call their earthly parent "my father," recognizing him as their progenitor and source of being, but in this case, we recognize "our father," — the common source of all life and our own included.

"Who art in heaven." It matters not whether we have in mind a special locality, or the perfected state of spiritual existence, we can at least all agree that there is a state where all the inhabitants know and do the will of the highest perfectly. Let us call it "Heaven," "Nirvana" or "Spirit-world," we all agree that there is a state where souls' have come to a knowledge of God's Laws or Mind, or both, and live in perfect harmony with those laws and therefore enjoy great happiness. The Buddhists labor and greatly deprive themselves, to gain that state which they call nirvana; and Christians do the same to gain heaven.

"Let thy kingdom come." We know what a kingdom is; it implies a king to whom all are subject, one whose will is the law of the land, a general ruler. The will of all kings is not worthy to be supreme; but in this case we desire that "Thy will be done," that this will be recognized as the one supreme law, "In earth as it is in heaven," so that all may act, speak and think, in harmony with it, and transgression against that supreme law cease. But say some, "that cannot be: even our devout Christian friends say this, yet they pray, or use these words in the attitude of prayer, every Sunday, without really expecting what they ask." To these

I add: "your Bible expressly says, 'Without faith it is a sin;' and a man asking a man for that which he did not believe he either would or could give him, would be truly a hypocritical mockery."

Jesus, who is accepted as the Son of God by Christians, as a great master by Buddhists, and as a wise teacher by all, recommended this prayer; the Rosicrucian's of the seventeenth century found in it the key to their mystic powers.

Not only do we read in the Hebrew Bible that God never changes, but reason itself teaches us that the great first cause must be the same forever; and, being the cause, must be ever present in all effects. How wise then were the words of David, Psalms, 139, vii. verse, "Whither shall I go from thy Spirit? If I take the wings of the morning, and dwell in the uttermost parts of the sea; even there shall thy hand lead me, and thy right hand shall hold me." Yes, truly, God is Spirit, and everywhere present.

This prayer is not uttered with any hope, or desire, to change God, but with the purpose to change ourselves. Desire, as we have shown in previous articles, is the natural process of growth; and is in the hands of the soul, by which it reaches out, and secures the food it needs. But need governs the desire, and uses the supply; therefore, to unite in a prayer for anything we do not feel the need of, or believe in, would not be prayer, and to pray for anything we do not use, would be an act without reason.

Then the prayer "Let Thy kingdom come, and Thy will be done on earth," implies a desire that we ourselves may be absolutely under the control of the will of "our Father" — God; and that is a state of entire submission and obedience to His will, to do, and be, whatever the promptings of the spirit require, thus justifying the words, "As many as are led by the spirit of God, they are the sons of God." Jesus claimed no more; he said, "I can do nothing of myself, the Father that dwelleth in me, he doeth the works."

The Rosicrucian's and oriental mystics claim that it is by coming into harmony with, and being governed by, the Spirit, that they possess their mystical power.

There are many today who are very desirous of becoming "masters," but there is only one true way for all, and that way is fully expressed in this prayer. True, there is what is called ritual or black magic, which is enacted by the carnal will and is destructive to the life and happiness of the practitioner; but this prayer, if dwelt upon day and night continually, will bring more changes for good than we can now realize.

Let us analyze it a little further. First, we are told in the Bible that God created man in his own likeness and image; and if God is our father, then we must possess the same nature and attributes that he has.

Considering the words, "Hallowed be thy name," — 'to hallow,' Webster says, is "to make sacred, to set apart for religious USE." Then, what is this name? — Zachariah says, "The Lord of hosts is his name;" the original Hebrew says, "Yahweh of hosts is his name." The best authorities all unite in that being the correct rendering and that its meaning is the WILL, or more literally expressed,

"I WILL BE, WHAT I WILL TO BE."

Thus, this name of God is the universal WILL, that has in itself power to will and do, and nothing can alter, change or hinder its mandates. This is the cognomen of "Our Father," the originator of all things. So then there is not, nor can there be, any power in the universe but that Will. — If we wish the assistance of that Will, we first recognize the source of our being, and desire to be in harmony with its Will for proper use and service. See the service Jesus rendered to the peoples, in healing the sick, casting out evils, raising the dead, etc. When we consider the laws and workings of our own body and mind, being in the likeness and image of our father, we thereby get a good idea of God. First a man is what his will makes him, — or he is what he wills to be. The Will is the absolute monarch of the body, we cannot move a muscle without its consent. God is the Will of the universe and must be correspondingly absolute. God is Spirit. We are here, confined in matter: do we want to be under the control of the WILL of our father? We cannot "flee" from it; we can simply disobey and suffer; for disobedience is the cause of all suffering, disease, and death. Therefore, to be in harmony with that Will is peace, happiness, health, and life.

Then, can we not all unite in this prayer from the soul, each making it a matter of personal effort? The nation is made up of individuals; and if each individual is in perfect harmony with God's will, then all the people will be.

So, the work of ushering in the kingdom is a personal one; and no one ought to wait for another, for if all should do so, nothing would be accomplished; but if each, independent of the other, works as though he were the only one, who was hindering the coming of that divine harmony into this earth condition, the work would soon be done.

Now, to our Christian friends, we would say, "faith without works is dead." Let us then all unite in faith and works, and pray, "Our Father who art in heaven, hallowed be Thy name, let Thy kingdom COME in me, let Thy will be done in my earth body as perfectly as it prevails with the holy ones in heaven." Let it be the expression of every breath, — "O to be psychologized [if you please,] by the will of God" "O, that it may control me in every thought, act, and desire!" And if that is the one real desire, we will all draw in, "inspire" the will of God until God will penetrate every attribute of our nature; then our Will and the universal Will will be one, all things will obey our will because all things obey the Will of God. This would constitute you a true master, and would enable you to say as we are told, Jesus said, "All power is given into my hands in Heaven and on Earth of my Father." Then your mind will be led into all truth, and by faithful obedience to its guidance, you would be led into a consciousness of the Spirit; that consciousness would enable you to see that God is in you, and around you on every side. Your Spirit eyes would see, your finer senses would feel the Divine Substance; and, lo! You would behold that God and Heaven are right here and you knew it not.

There are many efforts being made in different directions to bring about a unity of thought and action. But there is only one way to accomplish that oneness (unity means oneness.) God the Spirit is one; his Will is one; and all who are one with that Will, will be of the one body. Now we ask all persons who desire a higher condition on earth to unite with us every Wednesday evening commencing May 9th. 1888, from 8 to 8:30, in silent soul prayer that we may all become one with the will of God, and be led, guided, and controlled by Him in EVERYTHING, dedicating ourselves and all we are, or wish to be, to God's will.

Remember, God cannot be influenced by any selfish motive, therefore, if you unite with us in this effort, you cannot make conditions for God's will to submit to. It is for you to surrender ALL to God, and it matters not what your idea of God is; we ask you to unite in this prayer to your own highest ideal, and if it is too narrow, your ideal will be expanded until the true ideal will be realized.

Therefore, earnestly follow the light you have; reaching up for conjunction with the will of God, that you may come into true unity with your fellow man, and thus promote the Divine Humanity on earth.

THE DEVELOPMENT OF THE RACE
Delivered before the Society Esoteric of Boston

Dear friends, I have thought this afternoon that perhaps it would be more profitable just to have a little quiet talk in regard to the uses and methods for obtaining a higher state of mental development. We are in a country where educational culture is held as preeminent, and every effort is being made to obtain knowledge from books, thereby making research into the knowledge that has been obtained in the past. All these things are good and useful, but, of course, limited. All that pertains to the knowledge of the past, belongs to retrospection and gathering the knowledge and experiences of those who lived in prior times. We know full well that we are in an age of progress. The human mind is unfolding, reaching out broader and deeper, penetrating the heretofore unknown, discovering the fields of usefulness as well as of understanding, and every new discovery that comes to the world is not limited in its effects to that one department, but opens out many other lines of knowledge, because everything that is, is governed by one universal and divine law.

The most of us unite in the belief that God is the Creator of all things, and those of our friends who may not, will agree in this, that all things spring from one common source or cause. Thus, all laws, all that pertains to the methods of nature's workings, must necessarily originate from one common source. Therefore, all laws must, of necessity, be the emanation of the one creative mind that projects all things into being. That being so, every invention, every new discovery, must of necessity open out new avenues by which we may be enabled, (if we utilize the opportunities which are placed before us,) to obtain broader and more perfect comprehension of the methods and objects of creation.

In my recent studies, I find that all the ancients who have written, or have made high attainments in the world, have been centralized on one point, viz: the laws governing creation. They have discovered that all things, no matter what they are, emanate from the law of creation. Any mechanical instrumentality is only an appliance of certain laws in nature, to cause some force to serve our purposes. We stop for a moment and look out into the world and see all kinds of machinery and all the inventions of art to beautify the world. It all originates in the inventive mind in its efforts toward the laws of creation, by applying those laws that govern the universe. The watch that you carry in your pocket represents very perfectly the movements and workings of the great time-piece of eternity, the movement of worlds or planets in their orbits. Everything that belongs to art is only an imitation of nature. Look wherever an attempt has been made to beautify, and you see in it an effort of the human mind to imitate nature. We look upon the walls; the pictures, the flowers of the paper are only the effort of the human mind to imitate creation. Thus, if we sum up all that belongs to human invention, human projections, we see in it all only a faint effort towards imitating the God of creation.

So, if we go still further back into nature, still further into the causes of things, we will then find out more perfectly the laws that govern all that there is in nature. We know that all the five senses, viz: seeing, hearing, feeling, tasting, and smelling, relate to the perception of material objects. We do not see the cause which produces them, we only see the thing produced. We watch the growing corn for hours and can see no growth; yet hour by hour, it grows from within. By what means? By an invisible and unknown power; something beyond the sensuous comprehension. There must be something in the mind of man that is capable of reaching beyond the physical sense before he can know the causes of the things that are. Therefore, to even approximate to an understanding of realities, we must of necessity go beyond the external senses.

The education of our day has been wholly that of the senses, and not only so, but the education has been against all that belongs to the occult, because of the bad use that has been made of them in the dark centuries that we have been passing through. Our teachers have all united in teaching the children that all such matters are the results of ignorance and superstition, until we have a civilization the most materialistic that has ever existed upon this planet. There never was a time in the history of the world when the people were so wedded to the physical as at this very hour. At the time that the Nazarene came to ancient Israel, they were not so benighted in this direction as we are today, while they were more ignorant in all other directions. At that time almost the only science that existed was occult science. Israel always had their prophets; and their counselors, and, whenever they wished to make any great move, would send for those prophets to guide them in that movement. But later, and until our times, there has been a constant struggle to crush out of existence all those spiritual powers in every direction, and to ignore the capacity of man to perceive and to be conscious of the creative mind.

This has had its use. I am not among those who are disposed to blame or censure. There has been a use. During this period of the world's darkness, you will find by examining of the brain formation of the people of today, and comparing it with the brain of the people four hundred years ago, that there has been more rapid development of brain power than in any period of the earth's history. The brain has been thrown forward, whilst prior to that time the greater portion lay back of the ear. During the time when the predominance of the brain was behind the ears, man ruled the world by brute force. We find in the majority of men today two-thirds of the brain in front of the ear. What does this teach us? The world has been growing in reason; and through its constant exercise, has developed the reasoning powers. We have, as a people, developed into the intellectuals to that extent that the laborers and mechanics are incapable, as well as indisposed to perform the amount of hard labor that our grandsires did. Those only who have not this development, are the men who like to do this laborious work.

The reasoning faculty of the brain is good because it enables us to understand the laws of God. Everything is necessary, and everything will be made of use; it is a good thing to know how to use to the best advantage the capacities which we have developed. The power of the reasoning faculties is promoted by methods of experiment. Our whole life has been an experiment. A mechanic who makes an invention tries many times before he succeeds. In every man's life, how many experiments are made before he succeeds? In every circumstance, we find that we are so conditioned that almost everything we do is an experiment. All the powers of the man are called into being by a life of experiment.

The work of developing man from a lower to a higher state of being has been going on with tremendous rapidity during these years. But now we realize that the time of experiment is a time of suffering, a time when the whole world is in a state of fermentation as the result.

What shall be done? is the question in the minds of thousands. One class of men is rising against another; the poor are blaming the power of capital for oppressing them, and on the other hand capital turns round and charges laboring men with indisposition to work. Both are right and both are wrong.

Experiment, which is the method by which knowledge comes into the world, has done its work. But now the time has come for solving the final problem of life, and the most highly developed class of minds in the world have seen the necessity of turning their attention towards the cause of these things. It is to that class of minds we must look for our salvation from a time of chaos and bloodshed, and through that class of minds alone, we shall find it.

All men and women possess capabilities in themselves, — if they but know how to apply them, if they but make efforts to develop and bring them into service, — that will enable them not only to inspire new thoughts from the spheres above, but even to rise into the sphere of the mind of the Creator and Cause of all things, and foresee and foreknow how these things are working, what is necessary to be done; and through that power of mind, they will be enabled to see and understand the laws and methods that should be applied to bring order, harmony and peace into the world.

Now this idea of being able to foresee and foreknow is in great disrepute. At once the world says that it is "fortune-telling," that it is all a myth and nothing in it, because we have had a long period wherein the world has been taught to look at things in that light. The most of the books that were intended to educate the mind of man in occult knowledge, have been collected and burned in the old world, and thus the means that the world once had of obtaining the knowledge and development of these interior powers have been destroyed as far as it could possibly be done. Whilst occultism is often mixed with superstitious notions, yet no person can believe in and try to utilize these interior and spiritual powers that every man possesses without obtaining some truth, from the fact that God is spirit, and the spiritual life in man is a part of God, is divine. Now "divine" means the power to foresee or foretell events, and the divinity that is the life of every organism, and animates and actuates every human creature, only needs the opportunity to spring forth and lead man on in paths of peaceful harmony and success.

I have told you before and can repeat here, that there is no man or woman that has made great attainments even in a business line, but has done it through that divination called Intuition, through which they have foreseen and deemed how the results of their acts would terminate. Some of them have received this through perception. Just as a psychometrist will take a letter or glove and, through perceiving the person who wrote the letter or wore the glove, tell all about him. Persons who have these powers fully developed, as soon as a business is mentioned to them, perceive just how the thing would turn out. If you ask them how they know, they may say they have followed their reason; for they do not know what their power is. There are others who have had an intuition which seemed to spring up in their mind, and they have a dear idea of what a certain act will terminate in. You ask them about it, and they say they know it will turn out thus and so. They may give you some reasons; but really, it is the intuition only that has instructed them. There are many methods by which an individual may have been led, and thereby have succeeded.

Why is it that divination, the God principle in man, should have been so degraded as we see it in some persons that have taken the position of fortune-tellers? We find them very low in their character. Why is it? It is this: God the spirit is creating through his spirit descending into matter. God descends into matter through generation. The generative principle in man is the point where God materializes himself. Now, if conditions are such that this principle is degraded to a low state, then the spirit that meets the man or woman on that plane of life will be the divine in its lowest element; for, as said above, divinity is all that there is in the universe, where it is manifested in different degrees, uses, and stages. Persons giving up their mind to low sensual practices, and at the same time trying to use those powers being active only on that plane of consciousness, become conscious of nothing but that which belong to that plane. In this way, fortune-tellers have cursed the earth by causing people to class all manifestations of spiritual power with their low practices so that they are called outlaws who give up to these influences for gain's sake.

All that, however, only tells us that there are such laws and such powers, and that these powers may be developed and conducted in an exalted way, as it was by the prophets of old. We all accept the prophecies that have been made in Bible times, because the minds of the prophets were elevated. They elevated every attribute of their nature in order to come into a consciousness of the divine in themselves in its highest and holiest conditions. The churches for all these years have been devoid of this, for they failed to go down to the bottom of these matters. The word holy spirit means the separate spirit, that spirit, which is not involved in matter, in your bodies, and bound to serve the uses of the physical; it is that more exalted and perfected mind power of divinity by which the causes of all the phenomena that take place in the world, are known, and understood, and controlled. Therefore, when we have united with, and come into a consciousness of that holy spirit, then we are in the consciousness of the mind which is the producing cause in this world, and then we shall be true prophets of God.

The animal world, to a certain degree, is wiser than we are. They are more in harmony with the mind of the Creator than we are; they know what we do not. If the farmer, when he is working in the fields, sees the wild geese flying south, he knows that there is a cold wave coming, because he knows that they are going away from it for self-protection. We are all familiar with a multitude of ways in which the animals know more than man. What is it in them that gives them this knowledge? It is the divinity whose voice has not been silenced, that has not been suppressed by experimental reasoning and is free to act itself. In other words, the animals being purely natural, and without reasoning power, which is the experimental, are obedient to the interior guidance of the spirit, — the same as Adam and Eve were in Eden before they found in them the desire to experiment; for this is the meaning of eating of the tree of knowledge of good and evil; upon the tree of experiment the fruits of knowledge grow. Now the animals are led by that pure mind of the universe. They have not set up their reason against those quiet leadings of the soul, but they follow it purely. Experiment has caused man to reject this, therefore man does not act as wisely as the brute creation.

Man is the only creature upon our planet that really disobeys the laws of the universe, or that suffers as much. Man, as long as he follows reason, which belongs to the senses, as has been said, must be in darkness, his life a life of experiment and the life of suffering; but as soon as he has subjected his reasoning to the interior intuitional, then he has found Eden again.

All this experiment was necessary that we should have knowledge; but it would not have been were it not for the hope of enjoyment and to escape suffering. It is a mystery to our minds to see persons spending their life-time in a sphere of action that to us would be suffering, and yet they seem to enjoy it; their will drive them into that sphere of life; they enjoy that which would make you suffer; simply because their innermost need is such that they cannot get the will to make any experiments in the line of your life, wherein you find pleasure and enjoyment which is to you much superior to theirs. Their enjoyment is on the plane that would bring to you suffering. All enjoyment and pleasure is relative.

The only absolute principle in nature is that which relates to cause. Provided we were unfolded in the spirit so that we had the capacity of turning our senses out of the natural or physical body, and could foretell and foresee all the events that would take place in an age to come, they would not even then approximate cause. Beyond that, there is another sphere of divinity, another sphere of cause as much superior to that as this would be beyond the sphere of our present capacity. To me it is a great consolation to know that I can go on with all the powers of my being, to know and understand the workings of creation, and by and by, when I have finished my work in the physical world, to step into the spiritual world where I shall be able to understand more perfectly. But then I will be only commencing in my real capabilities of knowing; though I should go on through all eternity in obtaining knowledge, yet I should never exhaust the fountain.

There are many who, as soon as they get one new idea, want to come before the public at once and begin to teach, when they really need to be taught. Those spiritual subjects are of grave import, and to teach them, one should know all about them from personal experience; we need to do as the oriental sages, withdraw from the world and live quietly where the powers of comprehension and understanding can traverse freely the realms of knowledge and experience, bask in the sunlight of divinity. Then heaven would begin on earthy and a heaven surpassing that of ancient Eden might be enjoyed here. We know that if we can get the mind of the people to look into those laws that govern their own beings, and begin to develop their own powers; in a single seven years, many of these mature minds before me this afternoon might reach that state, where, if they should go out from the world and dwell in that spiritual thought, they would have obtained mental powers, so that such isolation would enable them to return to the people with all the abilities needed to lead others into that same divine harmony and heaven: whereas in remaining here among the people, subject to all their vicissitudes, they could never become conscious of the divine harmonies, enough to enable them to lead others also into them. We intend to picture the path to light and life so plainly in the course of lectures on "The Narrow Way" that notwithstanding all the struggles and anxieties with which we are all surrounded we shall be able to walk in that path, and reach the goal. The length of time that it takes us to reach the goal will depend upon ourselves, on the amount of devotion that we are willing to give to the work, which means that, if we wish to make rapid strides in these attainments, we have got to promise obedience to the guidance of the spirit of God, ever desiring to know the truth that we may do it and be qualified to lead others into it. Where this devotion is most active, the most knowledge will be obtained. The vital principle of life is loving devotion. In order to obtain the consciousness of God, we have to promise implicit obedience to the guidance of the spirit, the spirit that speaks in the soul.

When we can understand the law of life, the laws which first gave us birth into existence, and apply them in harmony with the divine mind of wisdom, then suffering, crime and misery will all pass away; self-condemnation and combat will cease. The understanding will be unfolded, and we will again begin to realize the divine inspiration of knowledge, wisdom, and power. These will make a higher degree than we are now capable of even thinking.

Through the development of this inner consciousness will be fulfilled the word of Obadiah, verse 21st., "And Saviors shall come," etc. For such have been the saviors of the nations in all the history of the past. Our present civilization is a mere mockery to the truly intellectual people of our age, and unless something comes to take the place of the present social and political condition, desolation is inevitable.

But we are not discouraged; there are many who are awake to these things and are desiring to know the way; and the world is not without its living lights to guide the people; and though all the records of the knowledge of the ancients were destroyed, it would still find living expounders.

Truth is indestructible and is ever waiting at the door of all who are ready to come in and be saved from anxiety, worriment, sickness, pain and death: for, as the Bible says of God, "Thy word is truth," that "word that liveth and abideth forever," is the only Savior.

IMMORTALITY; CAN IT BE OBTAINED WITHOUT DEATH
AN OPEN LETTER

The reported interview, which appeared in the Boston Globe and New York Herald of Sunday, April, 8th under the head of "Immortality, can it be obtained without death?" so materially differs from the statement we actually made, that we infer the reporter must have undertaken to supplement inadequate notes by memory and imagination, and as a number of letters have been sent us relative to the views expressed, we perceive that there must be a lively interest in the subject. We would accordingly present our real views, as on a question of such vital interest we do not like to be misunderstood. Our claims in brief are as follows:

All-natural law is unchangeable; such being the case, the same law that gave us our present existence, enabling us to develop from childhood to manhood, can be so applied as to enable us to go on developing this manhood into a higher and more perfect state of existence. We are of those who hold all life to be immortal; and that, as we possess in our bodies the power to create, or gather and give quality to life, we have also the power to hold and control it by our own will. Again, we know that the mental and physical power is in accordance with the quality and quantity of life, and that the thought directs and controls the life and causes it to do service in any direction the will decrees. But as all will power is derived from God, who gave his "name" according to the Bible as Yahweh which means Will and as that will is the energy of all life, — to embody it, the mind of man must first be harmonized with the God will, and thus made in harmony with all nature. Then all unnatural struggle and anxiety will have passed away. It is well known that anxiety and worriment cause premature age and infirmity. If an aged man can produce young life in an offspring, transmitting the capacity to develop vigor and manhood, then he must contain in himself the power to "regenerate" and renew his own youth and vigor.

It is, we believe, accepted by all scientific men that every particle of the material of the body is thrown off and replaced by new ones within seven years. If this is so, then the mental consciousness is the only permanent attribute of man. Physicians say to a depleted patient: "you lack vitality (vita, life); you need to feed up and get more strength," — thus recognizing the fact that we gather life through feeding the body. And it is as well understood that all mental and physical actions exhaust the life; for if one stops eating, he cuts off the life supply, and the material of the body is consumed, so that flesh is reduced as well as strength. Thus, it is manifested that the amount of life determines the amount of flesh supported by it; and it is true, as Dr. Hammond says, could we bring about equilibrium between the supply and the exhaust, life might be perpetual, providing the mind, — which is the only perpetual principle — could avoid all thought that produces destructive conditions in the body. For if the mind is the only permanent principle, then it follows that it is the mind that governs the rebuilding of the body, and also controls the quality of the chemical elements incorporated into the body to be perpetuated. Therefore, youthful growing life may be created in us, but the mind must be in perfect harmony with God, before that state can be reached; for if God is the Creator of all things, then all laws must be the product of the mind that created it — the Mind of God; and all that there is in scientific knowledge is but a knowledge of Creation.

There is a quality of life that is inexhaustible, which is often intact when persons are in the last moments of earth life; even when the body is emaciated, with not strength enough to move a muscle, the mind is often clear and lucid. This is from the quality of life that Jesus the Christ called regenerate, i.e., that which is generated in and reabsorbed by the body, being like the original germ from which, the body came. When this law is correctly understood and applied by the will, the power of life and death will be in our possession the same as it was with Jesus. He not only said but demonstrated in his death and resurrection, that "I have power to lay down my life, and have power to take it up again." This power, said Jesus, "I received of my father;" — and is not God our father too? The Bible tells us we are the sons of God; can we not then obtain the same power? Or is God partial to some? We are trying through the columns of the Esoteric to lead the thoughts of the people into the knowledge of the divine laws, which must be both scientific and religious. The Bible is full of passages that can only be interpreted as teaching the possibility of immortality in the body.

SUGGESTIONS OF THOUGHT FOR MUSINGS

The light-rays that come to earth bring with them the thought essences from stars, planets, and suns; bring with them the qualities of races unknown and unknowable to mortals here on earth; for every star is peopled with inhabitants diverse from all that is known on earth. God in his infinite wisdom makes each world a part of every other world, and some of the qualities that cannot be received by the mind of man in the present low stage of development of our earth, are taken up by the fruits and vegetables, plants and flowers, also by insects, and the waters of the ocean, as the germs out of which, in the eons yet to come, there will be developed like minds, feelings, thoughts, and emotions.

We have said in former articles that in involution the elements intended for the development and growth of the inhabitants of earth descended through man down through the lower orders of life, but if this were true in the absolute, or rather if this were the only way earth received any of these elements, there would be found on our planet nothing but what was good and wholesome for man's use; but there are found many poisons, and elements which would produce marvelous changes in the human system, if brought into contact with it. In many cases this is because they contain elements and qualities that man is not yet capable of receiving and utilizing; for our planet earth is still in a low stage of animal development.

Even the most highly developed man or woman upon our planet is but gross animal compared with the grand souls that walk the planets and suns that sparkle in our heavens. Many cycles of development must yet come before we can compare with those who dwell in some of the dim worlds that float in space, and what could we say of those souls who inhabit those brightly radiant suns that illuminate our night? We know but little more about the universe in which we live than the grasshopper knows about the mind of man.

"When I consider thy heavens, the work of thy fingers, the moon and stars, which thou hast ordained: What is man that thou art mindful of him? and the son of man that thou visitest him?"

For an illustration, let us consider for a moment, Sirius, that beautiful star which adorns the heavens during the winter season. By the aid of most powerful telescopes, astronomers have discovered that around it revolves a world whose volume is so immense that it would take 7 suns the size of ours to equal that one world: and we can form only the vaguest idea when we begin to consider that Uranus is 70 times larger than our earth, Neptune 100 times larger, Saturn 700 times larger, Jupiter 1300 times larger, while Mars, Venus and Mercury are smaller: yet all these balls, or planets, might be laid side by side, touching each other, and they would not fill a space or form a line reaching from the circumference of our sun more than one fourth of the way to its center; yet the sun is only one seventh of the bulk of one of these planets of Sirius, and what then must be the bulk of Sirius?

Then stop and consider the fact that worlds grow, and according to their size is their age, and according to their age is the state of their development and mental unfoldment; and as worlds grow, they incorporate added qualities, which become part of the race. From this, the greatest minds of earth can form but a vague estimate of what wonders of mind exist in the universe; and all this mind grows from God, as the tiny branch grows from the mighty oak. Now, as we live under the influence of these wondrous mind-powers, how important it is that we should avail ourselves of every facility offered us to increase our capacity to receive, know and understand these gigantic minds of other worlds.

Why, dear friends, could we but meet face to face some of the lowest men of those grand suns that float in space, their dignity, grandeur of mind, excellence of quality, and wonderful luminous soul powers would transcend our highest idea of God — Divinity itself. How small we seem when we "consider the heavens" — God's heavens; when we know that our earth is a little dark grain of sand compared to the worlds and systems of worlds that float in space.

Up to the present time, the inhabitants of our world have been ruled the same as are the beasts of the forest, by brute force. Look at England,

Germany, France, Russia, and all the great nations, armed with their floating batteries and mighty guns, intimidating and holding in check each of the other by virtue of their power to kill and destroy! Each animal fights for mastery, and when he has obtained, it keeps ever prominent his power of conquest. All the great nations of the so-called civilized world are doing the same as the barnyard rooster, only they have used mind-power to obtain facilities to destroy life more quickly and effectually, but they are applying the same law.

Now the time has come that our race has developed to where a higher law must obtain. The last great struggle of all nations is now upon us, in which they will find from experience — which is the only teacher — that force of arms is not the true method of perpetuating peace and tranquility, but that a higher law must be recognized and received: that law taught by the humble Nazarene, expressed in the words; "Peace on earth, good will toward men;" and that instead of fighting like the lowest hoodlums and destroying each other, the mind must be enthroned. Reason — not of the animal, sensuous nature — but of the higher spiritual nature must be enthroned, and when it is thus enthroned, then men and women will see that the root of all the evils which infest our fair earth is the abuse of that one God given principle: sexual generation.

When that is rectified by men and women living the regenerate life, then will there awake in the soul of man a consciousness of the mind of his God, and he will realize that all are brethren. Then peace and harmony will reign supreme because God is our Father, and from Him, or It, we draw all mind qualities, all conscious thinking powers. When these powers are merged in God, because of the capacity to realize the wonders which lie before us in the work of evolutionary development, and the fact that each mind is affected by every other mind, then it will be observed that peace and tranquility can be maintained only by complete harmony with the mind of the Creator.

But before this glorious time can obtain on our planet, the majority of the human race will destroy each other, because we are now in an age in which materialism predominates. Gold is God; therefore, in order to cleanse the earth and prepare it for the nobler race which is to begin the new cycle now to commence upon it, the inverted and unfit of the human family must destroy their own physical bodies.

We said that brute force ruled the world, and if that condition must be destroyed in order that the higher may come in, then it follows that all of these individuals who are active in perpetrating this rule must physically perish and pass away and be taken from the structure in earth form; and in the accomplishment of this, all rulers, as such, with every government and institution protected by that government, must perish and pass away, and the words of the angel to John the Revelator; will be literally fulfilled when he said; "And God shall wipe away all tears from their eyes; and there shall be no more death, neither sorrow, nor crying, neither shall there be any more pain: for the former things are passed away." And he that sat upon the throne said, "Behold, I make all things new."

SIGNS OF THE TIMES

We have now come to the closing scenes of another year. We know what experiences it has brought to us in the external and physical, but as the cause always precedes the effect, we do not know what lines it has marked out for us for the year to come. The year that is now past has been one of the greatest uncertainties. As the prophet said when he received the vision, "I saw, but I understood not," so it has been with all classes of people throughout the world, and especially in America. But what we have seen is only the preparation for the final great struggle that is now pending in the world. We believe there has never been a time when so much has been said of peace, and at the same time such strenuous efforts made to prepare for war. There have been several international alliances; which means simply the unity of military and naval powers against opposing nations; and owing to the success of this unity, England contemplates the expenditure of immense sums to increase her army and navy. All nations seem to feel that the time has arrived for a great and mighty struggle, and truly it has. As we view the conditions of the world now, honor has forsaken the nations, justice has retired into seclusion, and righteousness is despised; therefore, the reaction has begun.

Let us see if we can make a picture of this. Suppose we draw an immense circle, and call that within it the earth. We draw within that circle a great multitude of vines, filling the entire sphere, but all these vines growing from four central roots. When winter approaches, the life-giving sap is drawn from the leaves and extremities of the vine, and concentrates in the larger trunks, until it ends in the root from which it started. This, we think, is a picture of the world in its present condition. All men, according to the symbology given in the Bible, and according to physiologists, sprang from four distinct sources or roots, classified in modem times as temperaments.

The monetary interests in the world are the sap or blood of life; the winter frost is the cold selfishness which has characterized our entire political economy, for we have many reasons to believe that our political servants have sold us for gain. The statesmen of the older nations are vigilant and most watchful of each other as enemies, and the hand of bribery is not as potent as in America. Mother England knows the profligacy of her sons, and that it requires only a few dollars to purchase our lawmakers and cause them to grant anything that she may desire; consequently, she unites with and aids another, and more subtle enemy, in singing in the ears of the United States of America the lullaby song of "peace, peace," when, as the prophet says, "There is no peace." On the contrary, even mother England herself is bribing our lawmakers so as to rifle our treasury and leave us paupers.

Let us return to that vine which we have just pictured. The above condition is the frost that kills the vine; but this vine has greater vitality than those of the vegetable kingdom because this is the vine of Yahweh's planting, and its vitality is that of men and women who, though they are crushed to earth, will rise to avenge their wrongs upon their adversaries; and the mind will survive the potency of blood life. As the whole human family form in themselves the vine, we may call those at the outermost extremity of the branches the laborer, next the mechanic, then the merchant, then the speculator, capitalist, etc. As this blight has come, the past year has started the monetary blood toward the roots. Honest laborers during the past year have been running to and fro throughout the land seeking for a day's employment, but alas what a dark picture presents itself to them, and what will be the result when starvation stares in the faces of hundreds of thousands of intelligent, honest working men and women? We can depend upon it, they will turn upon those who are withdrawing the source of their supplies, follow the channels of the monetary vitality, and demand from thence a perpetuation of their means of subsistence. As this will be denied, the laboring classes will become like so many wolves, and when this begins to pinch and oppress the merchant, the speculator, etc., they will find that a den of tigers and lions has been disturbed, who, with fearless ferocity, will take and devour everything that comes in their way. To appease this and turn away its fury, the war of nations will come, which will be, in turn, only an organized force of destruction, instead of one which is unorganized, — but we will not dwell further upon this dark picture.

Our friends will remember that we called their attention to these things years ago, and tacitly advised them to put all their financial resources, as far as possible, into ready cash. But few persons have done this. Letters are pouring in upon us, expressing the desire of the people to come to us and become members of the Colony movement, but nearly all, with one accord, express the fact that they have lands and estates, which, so far as yielding ready cash is concerned, are worthless. True, they are worthless, and why? There have been a thousand times more money loaned, on which men are required to pay interest, than has ever been in the country; because the same money is loaned over and over again, until the interest per annum demanded for a hundred dollars is, in many cases, much more than the original sum. The ebb-tide has now begun to expose the nakedness of all those who have depended upon usury for support; and you may depend upon it, dear friends, the words of Paul have a special significance at this time; "Old things are passed away: behold, all things become new."

The past year has been one of marvelous preparation. The forces have been gathering; and concentrating on the destruction of all old things. Jesus said in his parable concerning the coming of the kingdom of heaven, that he would send forth his angels to gather the tares in bundles to be burned (destroyed), but would gather the wheat into his garner. Now, if this parable means anything, it means the separation of the one class from the other. There are multitudes who are represented by the wheat growing in the midst of weeds, — which might be called tares, — and when, from an intellectual standpoint, one examines these tares: weeds; they find so much good in them. Why, here in the West, the weeds and wildflowers are so numerous that the cattle feed and continue to eat upon the abundance of seed that lies upon the ground from their ripening, and is not this good? Those who are raising cattle for the market say, yes, it is; but those who would plant and subdue the land and cultivate it, say, no; they are the greatest evil with which we have to contend; they root out and destroy our wheat and absorb the vitality from our crops. So, it is in the time in which we live. We look around us, and we find that the masses of the people are in themselves good, but their goodness is like that of the weed and the wild flower; and as God is the great farmer, and we, his children, are the pleasant plants, he sends forth his angels with the proclamation: "Oh ye out of the midst of her that ye be not partakers of her sins!" The prophet said, (Jer. iii. 14,) "I will take you one of a city, and two of a family, and I will bring you to Zion;" for, throughout the land, the people have been so mixed up with the tares that there is seldom more than one of a family that are of the wheat. The time has come when that separation must begin. As the prophet Zechariah said, "In that day shall there be a great mourning as the mourning of Hadadrimmon in the valley of Megiddon. And the land shall mourn, every family apart."

Those who would save their friends and neighbors now, and be benefactors in general to the world, cannot do so by remaining with them; but will find themselves as weak and powerless as their neighbor, and needing help as much as they, for the time has come that the "Lord will do his work, his strange work, and his acts, his strange acts." We know this from the fact that the Lord appeared to us in January 1893, and showed us that the time had arrived, and in our presence sent forth his angels, as the executors of his will and the harvesters of the earth.

All who are obedient, cannot fail to perceive the rapid, onward progress of the judgment and harvest. Who among you is ready to cease from "man whose breath is in his nostrils: for wherein is he to be accountable?" and dedicate your life to God without reserve, and follow his guidance, no matter where it leads or what it costs you, even though it leads you to separate sensuous love, and to unite yourself with those whom you can only love with the spiritual and heavenly love.

From the beginning of the world to the present time (turn to the history and see) God's prophets have all been prophets of evil, and not of good to come to the world, as a body. These prophets have been crucified because of this: they have been stoned and compelled to live in dens, and in the secret places of the earth. Now that the time has come for the fulfillment of their burning words, those who dare to repeat them in your hearing are persecuted, and called crank and obnoxious prophets of evil, just as the prophets were who gave them voice in the beginning.

The coming year will be one of gathering in the ripe fruit of the earth (perfected souls), and the question comes to every one of you with greater importance than at the time when Jesus said to his disciples, "One of you shall betray me," and they all began with one accord to say. Is it I? Is it I?

Now let each begin to ask themselves concerning this most important matter of the people who are to be called out from the world and made the vessels of the Lord, Let them inquire; Is it I? Is it I? Is it I? for the prophet said, "Go ye out from the midst of her; be ye clean, that bear the vessels of the Lord." The time has come when the clean must be separated from the unclean, in order that God's kingdom may be established on earth; for the kingdoms of this world are now to become the kingdom of our Lord and of his Christ — the anointed body.

FAITH IN GOD

We presume there is no part of Christian doctrine that has been more abused through lack of knowledge than this one of faith in God. It has been believed that persons may obtain special favor of God and then he will take care of them and all that belongs to them. An illustration of this occurred in San Francisco. There was one there who had — or thought he had — such perfect faith in God that he would not lock his door when he went from home; but one day someone entered and carried off all that was valuable. Such instances are of frequent occurrence, because of those who argue that a Christian should take no precaution in the way of self-protection. These seem to be justified in the accounts set forth in the Bible of the prophets in ancient times. We also read in modern occult works of great masters who, through their spiritual powers, could turn away the hand of the assassin, and who were able to protect not only their own life and property, but that of other, without weapons of defense. Jesus said, "If thou canst believe, all things are possible to him that believeth." Is this contradicted by the experience of those who have lost their property, and sometimes their lives, while trusting in God's protection? It would be so were the faith required, purely of the reasoning mind, and only a sufficient quantity needed to cause men to act upon it. But this is not enough; the faith must be without a doubt, and this faith can only be attained through living the life which will produce it.

We are told that God created by the word of his power; therefore, he must have created from himself, as literally as a father and mother create offspring from themselves; and because of this fact we are the sons of God, as truly as we are children of our earthly parents. If this be true, then the laws of God's nature are necessarily the laws of our nature. As God never changes, therefore the laws of his nature must be complied with in our life, in order that we may be in harmony with God; and as God created all things, from the animalcule in the drop of water to the highest form of man, not only in this world but in all worlds, therefore it inevitably follows that all laws are God's laws. As God cannot look upon sin "with the least degree of allowance," — for man must reap that which he sows, absolute justice being the attribute of Deity, — therefore the soul of man is made conscious of every transgression of law, and made to feel that by virtue of that transgression justice will be meted out.

Now, man may reason his intellect into the belief that he is in Divine favor, and therefore will be protected under all circumstances by the power of the divine will; but that belief will not be without a waver or a doubt; because the soul of man cannot lie, and it is its province to protect and care for the body. It will therefore admonish the individual, no matter what arguments may be brought to bear upon the mind, of the fact that he is not living in harmony with divine law; and therefore, there will be doubts and fears continually active in the mind until the individual lives perfectly in harmony with these laws.

We read of Daniel being cast into the lion's den, and that he said the Lord had sent an angel and shut the lion's jaws, that they should not hurt him; but have we not reason to believe that this fact was governed by law? We read that Daniel and the three Hebrew children would not eat of the king's meat, that their food was exclusively pulse and grains. Now, it is well known in some of the mystic orders, and to individuals not associated with any of the orders, that the soul of man, through the compliance of the intellect, may make a covenant of peace with all life, or with the spirit of the life of the planet, to henceforth neither kill nor destroy, nor in any way partake of that which is killed; and that after sufficient time has elapsed for his own flesh to be changed — purified from the life of the animal — he will find that his soul and body are at peace with all flesh, and that the animal world is at peace with him. Then he may be cast into a den of lions, or into any other position of danger, and no harm to him will ensue. We hold that persons who are not keeping this covenant could not have sufficient faith in God to make them fearless under such circumstances; and if they were that, it would not save them from destruction. This is true of every condition in which man has a need for faith in God. He must live up to the requirements of the law, that he may not be under the condemnation of the law; then divine justice will manifest itself even through the wild beast.

Before man will be able to protect himself from the brutality of man, he must have conquered it in himself and risen superior to it. Then, and not until then, can he unite his will with the will of God, and be sufficiently imbued from on high with that infinite power to speak peace to the angry mind of an adversary and cause it to turn from its wrath. Thus, faith in God is an attainment, a gift — but not in the sense of God giving something to someone which had not been earned or possessed; for the angel paid to Daniel, "But the saints of the Most High shall TAKE the kingdom:" and Jesus said, "The kingdom of heaven suffereth violence and the violent take it by force." Neither of these declarations indicate that there are any especial favors to be given in that direction, but as Jesus said, "He that is ABLE to receive it, let him receive it." It follows, therefore, that every man who receives such powers is to take them by the application of law. God is not necessitated to change, but he has created all these laws; they exist everywhere, and when man has developed a sufficient power of mind — knowledge — to comply with the requirements (cease from sin) he will obtain the results, and as he obtains the results, that unwavering faith in God and his laws will come naturally to the individual. It will be an unwavering faith, because the soul will know that it has these powers, and when the reasoning mind tries to believe from without, the soul will confirm such belief from within, and such faith will cause the individual to say I know that such-and-such will be the result. This knowing is only faith, until actual experience has been obtained, but the confidence in it will be no greater after it has been proven than it was before. Therefore, in the consciousness of the individual, there is no difference between faith and knowledge. All true faith in the affairs of men is called by them, as a rule, knowledge. You ask one, "Can you do so and so?" the answer is an emphatic "yes;" then ask him, "Do you know that you can?" the answer will be "yes; I certainly do." But this, however, is not absolutely true, for it is faith until it is accomplished, and then it becomes knowledge; therefore, faith in God is only obtainable by living up to the requirements of the law until the soul consciousness becomes so confirmed by reason of realization in itself, that the individual is disposed to say, I know it will be done.

The Esoteric movement from the beginning has presented laws and methods which, if followed, will lead to these results. As we have said in former articles, use is a prime law in all nature; nothing can exist unless it be useful in the great economy of God's nature. Use cannot obtain without first a need; therefore, it follows that this movement was needed by the world, or it would not have come to it; and as that which is being accomplished by it is very great, therefore the use and need must be proportionately great.

We believe that there has never been a time in the history of the world when there was such a need for absolute faith in God. We are on the eve of trials and suffering's, through loss of property and life, greater than that of any preceding age. When the children of Israel entered the land of promise, God ordained that there should be cities of refuge to which men could flee and save their lives from the hand of the slayer. We believe this to be only the antitype of the present times, in which God will appoint cities of refuge into which His people may flee and be safe. There are thousands of men and women who dimly foresee the need of these cities of refuge, and through egotism, the desire for notoriety, are making the effort to build such cities; but all such cities, instead of being cities of refuge, will be the exact opposite. This does not, however, invalidate the fact, but rather substantiates it, that there will be cities of refuge appointed and protected by the God of heaven.

How are people to determine which is the false and which the true? We have heretofore given directions in this magazine concerning the covenant dedication of self and all that we have and are to God, and tried to impress the importance of obtaining this faith in God sufficient to cause you to follow the guidance of his spirit under all circumstances; for if there were cities of refuge built, how could you know which was the false and which the true ones unless it were by this faith in the guidance of God's spirit? Again, if a time of general disturbance and chaos is coming in the world, you will need the guidance of intelligence that knows all things, from the beginning to the end. The Esoteric movement has presented methods which, if carefully and perfectly followed, will lead all persons into a condition where they will have this absolute guidance.

There are many persons who expect to obtain this guidance as soon as they begin to live the life, but they find themselves awakening to a new and strange realm of consciousness, and although they have the guidance, yet they do not know how to distinguish between it and the new realm of thought-consciousness into which they have entered. This they must learn for themselves. Jesus said, "My sheep know my voice and follow me, but a stranger will they not follow, for they know not the voice of the stranger." When one first begins to hear the voice, it is the voice of the stranger, even though it be the voice of the spirit of the Highest, until they have learned to know that voice; for as soon as one begins to open into this new world, they hear many voices, and it is only from experience that they are able to distinguish between the voices of the mundane and the voice of the master. We repeat what we have so often said; that it is absolutely necessary for one to first dedicate their life, and hopes, and desires, and all that they have and are, to God, and to cultivate in their thoughts faith enough in God to believe that he will not leave them in darkness, but will show them the way; then, doing the very best, they know they have a right to expect that the Holy Spirit will make them know the right, and enable them to shun the wrong. Then if they live as near right as they know how, every day, they will have reflected upon their consciousness knowledge of truth, and by carefully watching and analyzing how these truths come to them they will soon be made to know that voice always. It does not always come to them as a voice; it frequently comes as faith. Therein is the word of the apostle true, that faith is the gift of God, and not of yourselves. It was by faith that Abraham was led for many years in the land that was promised to him and his children, and when this faith comes to you, you only feel as if you knew just what to do; and if you have been in the habit of following that faith, you will be well able to distinguish between the true and the false.

It is not surprising that it is so difficult to walk by faith in a land that is all skepticism and doubt. We are surrounded by multitudes of persons who have been taught from their childhood to deceive and the keenest intellects exhaust their powers in that direction. We have come to a condition where we really doubt our own senses, and it is not surprising that We doubt every inner prompting. It is because of this that it is necessary to "convert" (change our course) and become as a little child before God. Have you not seen parents take a little child that has not yet learned to walk and stand it upon a table and step back and hold out their hands to it? And the little thing would hold out its hands and fearlessly fall from the table into the parent's arms. Therein was expressed the perfection of childlike faith — the faith that we must have in God.

In many cases it is necessary before it is possible for us to have that faith that everything on earth on which we depend should be taken away from us, and we be forced to follow the guidance in sheer desperation. I presume it is because of this the prophet, voicing the word of God. said, "When thy judgments are in the world, the people will learn righteousness;" for it is true, that when we have all that heart can wish we feel no need of God's spirit to guide and keep us, and nothing would induce us to move from our place; but when our place becomes unbearable, then we, like the young eagles, seek another place. Moses said, "As an eagle stirreth up her nest, and fluttereth over her young, spreadeth abroad her wings, taketh them, beareth them on her wings; so, Yahweh alone did lead him, and there was no strange god with him."

That was not only a beautiful symbol of how God had dealt with his people Israel in Egypt, but a symbol of how God always leads and guides and deals with his people. It is said that an eagle always builds her nest of thorns, and then fills in between the thorns and covers them with a soft down. There she raises her young until they are old enough to fly. But the young eagles are lazy and will not leave that delicious nest where they are fed abundantly and have all that heart can wish; so the old eagle pulls out the soft lining of the nest and lets their little breasts down upon the sharp thorns, which makes the nest wherein they were raised unbearable; and so, by their own volition, they are forced to get out of it, and as they sit upon its edge, the mother eagle will push them off so that they find themselves suspended in mid-air, where they are forced to fly or fall. Then the old eagle flutters over them, and when the little ones get tired and are likely to fall, she flies under them, takes them upon her back and bears them up until they are rested, and so teaches them to fly. How like God's dealings with his people under all circumstances this is! Are the thorns making your nest unbearable? Then look to the parent spirit for guidance, that you may know what to do; then try to cast yourself — like the young eagle — upon the strong pinions of the King of spirits, and he will bear you up and direct your course to the city of refuge that he has builded. But none need seek that city of refuge who have not that faith in God that they can throw themselves upon his boundless love, wisdom and power, and expect to be upheld and guided by it, — none need seek that city merely as a place of support, or a place where they will be cared for, for it is because of that condition of mind that you are stirred up from your old nesting-place and thrown out of it, so that you will obey the injunction, "Go work in my vineyard."

There are those who are so self-sufficient that they cannot cast themselves upon God until every possible chance of self-maintenance has been taken away; then many times all hope will have fled from them, and it will be forever too late.

May God's spirit impress you with the truth concerning your own position.

THE COMING KINGDOM

Through all time, the human mind has looked forward to, and idealized, a happy home and loving companionship. The loving disciple John said, "God is Love, and he that dwelleth in love dwelleth in God." That divine spark in the human breast causes this ideality, and as all knowledge is gained only through experience, the world has been experimenting on these divine principles until the majority of the human family have come to the conclusion that no human love can be continuous; and it has been debased into the grossest passion, until mere licentiousness has become so prevalent that many think it the normal course of life; and we believe there are, because of it, today, more unmarried men and women than in any other period of the world's history; certain it is that there are many more divorces. If we should say that this is because of a higher state of intelligence, it would no doubt call out criticism, but such is undoubtedly true; for all true intelligence arises from the consciousness of the soul.

It is well known to the mental philosopher that the physical brain cannot, and does not, furnish the knowledge that is possessed by the truly intellectual. The soul seldom forgets any experiences of its entire existence, while the brain is continually forgetting the past, and living in the present and future. This is right and good, and as God would have it; for to live in the past is to stop all progression. While the soul remembers the past it is only such of the past as is of use in the present; but the soul being nearer to the spiritual, can reach out into the fountains of the cause-world and gather in whatever of truth is necessary for the occasion.

That which has been denominated in the past as conscience, we, for the sake of a clear understanding, denominate the consciousness of the soul. The Bible says, "Whatsoever ye bind on earth is bound in heaven;" and this is a law which obtains under all circumstances; therefore, whatever a person believes with the intellect to be right or wrong is their law which they have made on earth, and is accepted as such in heaven until human experience demonstrates to their intelligence that it is not a correct law or course of life; then that course is condemned by their own soul, and is condemned in heaven for them, and their conscience will no longer chide them, unless they continue to lead that life which they know to be wrong.

Thousands of men and women throughout the land have become conscious that there is something wrong in the old marriage relations, notwithstanding their soul and all the feelings of the body eagerly reached out for it and caused them to realize it as the most sacred and holy relation of the human family. But if the soul so instructs them, and reaches out for it, why is it that the same conscience immediately afterwards condemns, and desires to be freed from it? The only answer that can be found is, the real object which prompted those holy desires was not understood, and was violated in every particular, and instead of God-like love binding them closer together, conscience condemns them and closes the door of loving sympathy to that kind of life. But as all their former teachings, and the thoughts, feelings, and desires of all their associates contradict the admonition of the soul-consciousness, and constantly condemn every thought of obedience to it, they are in a dilemma, and many live for years, condemning themselves for having such thoughts and feelings. But is it a condemnation of self? For when a person condemns the promptings of the soul arising from its recognition of divine law, such condemnation is not only of the soul, but of God and his laws. But the influence of surrounding minds, which continually condemn the higher law, reflects upon their mind condemnation for any feeling; or desire to leave the old, perverted order and enter the divine order, and causes them to feel that they are condemning themselves.

There certainly is no remedy for the rapidly growing conditions of base sensuality, except such as lies in a knowledge of the true, divine order. This, we, through The Esoteric, have been laboring to present to the world for the last seven years, during which time many homes which were discordant and unhappy have been made harmonious and comparatively happy, as will be seen in the testimonials which have appeared in the magazine during the last three years. This is not the most important object of our work, for it relates only to a higher and holier order of generation, which, however, is very necessary to be established in order to remove the present evils that are festering in the human family, and to bring into existence a higher order of men and women to people our planet. But among these is another class who have, through actual mental and soul development, reached a physical condition where it would be impossible for them to give a child a good, healthy body. For years, God, through his wise laws, caused the highly intellectual and spiritual natures to marry low, animalized natures, in order that there be an equalization in the human family, otherwise the gross would become grosser and the highly intellectual, finer; but development among our people has reached a height where intelligence governs them to that extent that they will not so unequally marry; and every man and woman whose intelligence has reached a degree of development where they are capable of and have a desire to understand these divine laws and methods which have characterized The Esoteric from the beginning, do, by that very fact demonstrate that they are incapable of giving offspring proper physical bodies. Therefore, we hold that this class of people, by those undeviating laws of evolutionary development, have no right to continue in the law of generation. Those who have a desire for marrying and raising a family of children, we believe that desire is prompted by the soul's consciousness that they are not only capable of producing good children, but that their work in that direction is not yet finished. But those whose desire — transcending all others — is to reach the highest goal of human attainment, are the ripe fruit of this age. To them we would say, there are heights and depths and breadths of knowledge, mind powers and accomplishments possible to you, now, in the world, transcending your highest imagination. Many of the occult books and novels tell us of men who have reached such high attainments that they are able to rule and govern in whatever sphere of life they are pleased to operate, and that they are able to command the elements of nature, heal the sick, cast out devils, and, in fact, do all the works we read of in Bible days, and furthermore, that these men set no value on gold and silver, except for its use for the day, and where they see fit to settle down in a home of their own they are surrounded by transcendent luxuries and elegance beyond that of the most wealthy. Now are these fables? or, are they a few of those things attainable? What did Jesus say of this? See Mark x. 29, 30., and John xiv. 12. Yes, we know that these conditions, and greater than these — for these belong only to the external appearances, but the thought-powers and the soul-consciousness have a value infinitely above all that earth can possibly give — are reached in the sixth degree of the order of Melchisedec.

None of these occult works which tell you of these things give you any idea of how they are attained, unless it be, perchance, through the methods of Hindu magic, or some other vagary that has no foundation. But we have come to you with methods from first to last, and methods which are so practical that everyone knows after taking the first step and onward, that they are real and practical and none of them merely ideal.

Now, if the first which we gave you have all proved true, have we not a right to claim your further attention, even though it contradicts some of the strongest impulses of your whole being? for have not those — the strongest impulses — deceived many of you in the old marriage relation? And now I tell you, who wish to reach the highest goal of human attainment, that if you marry, it will deceive you again; even though you idealize and determine to live that high and holy counterpartal life, yet it will deceive and turn your course into other channels. Now, remember, we do not forbid to marry, we only tell you that if you wish to reach the highest goal of human attainment on earth, you must wait until you know something of the high and holy condition referred to by that great and holy master, Jesus, when he said, "For in the resurrection they neither marry, nor are given in marriage, but are as the angels of God in heaven." If you wait and labor on until you obtain the resurrection, then you will know how the angels live, for you will see them and associate with them while here in the earth body. When Masonry was fresh from the hands of that holy Melchisedec, king of Salem — the house of God — that existed at the time of Abraham, it was understood that the resurrection, and the decomposition and throwing off the old, fleshly conditions was a work which must be accomplished by the neophyte before he was master; and there exists among them to-day a grip, and an allegory, which in that early age belonged to the fifth degree, — which it always will, for man cannot change that divine order. Masonry, as known in the world to-day, has been altered; its holy occupant cast out, and in place of truth and vitality has been installed error and ideality, and that old and sacred Temple is used as a place where bad boys may amuse themselves in play.

The time has come when God and his Holy ones are again to build that holy Temple, and the glory of this latter house will transcend the glory of all that hath preceded it; and you, dear children, who are striving for the highest goal of human attainment, are called to be builders of that house. Know this, that the high and holy condition with which your soul impresses you cannot be maintained on earth until that house is builded; and while you are climbing up through the first, second, third and fourth degrees, the life within you is getting more refined, and becoming more potent, and reaches out stronger and yet stronger in its desire for that ideal love and companionship, till you stand before the door of that royal fifth, and that which is allegorically expressed in the Master's degree becomes a realized fact to you, and you stand forth a resurrected man, holding the keys which are found in that great name of God. Then indeed you will open and no man can shut, and shut and no man can open, "for thou hast a little strength." So, hold on and hold out in your determination and your forward trend, for the gold you seek is worth more than all the treasures earth can give, of every name and nature. Neither is it so far from any of you, as some who are playing at occultism would have you think. We know one instance of one who reached the royal fifth in a little more than four years. If one can reach that point in that time, certainly others can.

When we discovered in our travels on this highway what magnitude and glories were to be planted on earth, and that they could not exist here under the present conditions, we determined to go before the people, tell them of that wonderful world that we had found, teach them of the roads that lead thereto, and thereby lead out a people from the slavery in Egypt into the promised land flowing with milk and honey, — which indeed is the glory of all lands, — and there build the temple, and make it possible for that glorious state which now exists in the heavens to perpetually exist on earth; for Yahweh, who cannot lie, has promised to set his name there and to dwell there with his people forever. But we wish to repeat what we have said to you before: This road grows narrower and more difficult all the way to that Holy City. The angel told Esdras it was so narrow that but one could pass at a time: so, if you contract to take one with you, the way will be found too narrow, and you will be compelled to stop. None but those who are able to tread that rugged path alone, unaided by other hands only as the light-bearer illumes the way, will ever be able to enter. As the ancient one said, "Naked we came into the world, and surely we can carry nothing out." But remember, he who brought the greatest light concerning this country said that though you give all for this attainment, you should receive a hundredfold in this present. He who said this, was poor, despised and afflicted of men, a man of sorrow and acquainted with grief; but he triumphed over death and defied the grave. Let us follow on; it surely is the best paying business in the end that every man or woman entered into; and there is no liability of failure, only in your wearying and turning aside, by the way.

When the angel showed John on Patmos those who had arrived at this holy city, he asked John, "What are these which are arrayed in white robes? and whence came they?" and Joint answered, "Sir, thou knowest;" and the angel answered him and said, "These are they which came out of great tribulation, and have washed their robes, and made them white in the blood of the Lamb. Therefore are they before the throne of God, and serve him day and night in his temple;" not a temple up in the sky, nor beyond the bounds of time or space, but in both time and eternity, and occupying space on the earth, where all saints have prayed for it to come during the last 1893 years; yes, all saints and prophets from the beginning of our age down to the present time, and thanks to God and his holy ones, these prayers are being answered with great rapidity. He that has begun the work is almighty, and NONE CAN TURN IT BACK.

AUTHOR AND MANAGING EDITOR

Darrell Jordan is an acolyte of the August Fraternity, former Noble Grand-IOOF and Freemason. He is also a member of the Theosophical and Philalethes Societies.

Darrell Jordan

BOOKS BY THE AUTHOR

- Illustrations of Masonry
- Surviving Document of the Widow's Son
- The Undiscovered Teachings of Jesus
- The Initiates
- Jefferson's Bible
- Master Masons Handbook
- Forgotten Essays - W.L. Wilmshurst
- Forgotten Essays - Waite
- Forgotten Essays - H. Stanley Redgrove
- The Writings of Sigismond Bacstrom M.D.
- Forgotten Essays – Reincarnation
- Masonic Writings of George Oliver
- Masonic Lectures by Wellins Calcott
- The Fellowcraft Handbook
- Secret Societies
- Vibration and Life
- Key to the Rosicrucian Characters
- The Revelation of John
- The Magic of the Middle Ages
- Musings of a Chinese Mystic
- The Life of the Soul
- Christian Mysticism
- Krishna and Orpheus
- The Eleusinian Mysteries & Rites
- The Crucifixion Letter
- The Mystic Key
- You Paid What?
- The Illustrated Pioneer History of the America
- Montana Freemasons 19th Century
- Washington Freemasons 19th Century
- Idaho Freemasons 19th Century
- Rock Metaphysics
- Emblems: Jean Jacque Boissard and Otto van Veen
- Emblems: Nicholas M. Meerfeldt
- Alchemy Art: Manly P. Hall
- Emblems: Manly P. Hall
- Alchemy Art & Symbols
- Splendor Solis

For the latest information, please visit author's book site: Parallel47North.com/collections/esoteric-books

If you have any question, suggestion, or feedback, please contact: info@Parallel47North.com

THE ARTIST AND ILLUSTRATOR

Hand-drawn Illustration of Hiram E. Butler and Book Cover Art by Jessica Naomi.

The Artist Portfolio: JessicaNaomiDesigns.com

Finis

www.ingramcontent.com/pod-product-compliance
Lightning Source LLC
Chambersburg PA
CBHW020309010526
44107CB00001B/41